To:

_____

From:

_____

Date:

_____

My
Pocket
Prayer Partner
for Women

HOWARD BOOKS
A DIVISION OF SIMON & SCHUSTER
New York   London   Toronto   Sydney

Our purpose at Howard Books is to:
- Increase faith in the hearts of growing Christians
- Inspire holiness in the lives of believers
- Instill hope in the hearts of struggling people everywhere
  Because He's coming again!

Published by Howard Books, a division of Simon & Schuster, Inc.
1230 Avenue of the Americas, New York, NY 10020
www.howardpublishing.com

My Pocket Prayer Partner for Women © 2007 by Dave Bordon and Associates, LLC

Library of Congress Cataloging-in-Publication Data

My pocket prayer partner for women.
    p. cm.
  1. Christian women—Religious life. I. Howard Books.
  BV4844.M93 2007
  242'.643—dc22

                                                            2007018682

ISBN-13: 978-1-4165-4217-9
ISBN-10:   1-4165-4217-5
10 9 8 7 6 5 4 3 2 1

ISBN-13: 978-1-58229-690-6 (gift edition)
ISBN-10:   1-58229-690-1 (gift edition)
10 9 8 7 6 5 4 3 2 1

HOWARD and colophon are registered trademarks of Simon & Schuster, Inc.

Manufactured in China

For information regarding special discounts for bulk purchases, please contact:
Simon & Schuster Special Sales at 1-800-456-6798 or business@simonandschuster.com.

Project developed by Bordon Books, Tulsa, Oklahoma
Project writing and compilation by Christy Phillippe, Betsy Williams, Rayné Bordon, and Shawna McMurry in association with Bordon Books
Edited by Chrys Howard
Cover design by Bordon Books
Permissions acknowledgments are on pages 216–217.

Contents

A prayer concerning . . .

Introduction

Who do you go to when you need to talk? To whom do you turn when you need encouragement? We all know that life is busy, stressful, and challenging. Yes, life can be difficult, but you can face anything when you know that God loves you and that He hears your cry for help.

This inspirational book, *My Pocket Prayer Partner for Women*, is packed full of resources to help you connect with the One who loves you most. Included are heartfelt prayers, inspiring reflections, and on-target scripture promises on fifty different topics. There is also a place for you to journal and record your thoughts or God's answers to your prayers. In the back of the book, there is a daily Bible reading guide to help you incorporate God's Word into your daily routine. You will gain a whole new perspective on life as you draw near to God and experience His love and grace.

God desires to be your confidante and your best friend. He is the only One who completely understands you, even when no one else does. So, pour out your heart to Him and ask Him for whatever you need today!

Tips for Having a Great Quiet Time

You may feel that the last thing you need is another commitment, but spending time with God is worth the effort. He desires to guide you, He wants to comfort you in the hard times, and He wants to be your friend. But He can only do that if you spend time with Him. The Bible says, "Draw near to God and He will draw near to you" (James 4:8 NKJV). Why not decide today that you will make Him a priority?

Here are some helpful tips:

- Give God your undivided attention. Find a quiet place where you and God can meet.

- Schedule a specific time. You are more likely to follow through.

- Read some verses from the Bible. Choose an easy-to-read translation. (You may want to use the Bible reading plan on pages 204–215.) As you start to read the Bible, ask the Holy Spirit to speak to your heart. As He impresses your heart and mind with His Word, why not pray those scriptures back to God? You may want to personalize those verses or paraphrase them in your own words. Praying God's Word back to Him is just one way that you can communicate with God.

- As you pray, also ask God for what you need. Keep a journal and record all the answers to your prayers. This will encourage you when you are down.

- The book of Psalms instructs us to sing to the Lord. Get a praise CD and sing along with it to your Heavenly Father.

- Talk to Him as you would a friend, from your heart. Then listen to see what He is saying to you. Remember, it is a relationship—it's not just you asking for stuff.

- If this is new to you, start out small, perhaps fifteen minutes. When you form the habit, you'll want to increase the time. As you get to know God even better, spending time with Him will go from discipline to desire to delight.

This book you hold in your hands is full of on-target promises from God's Word, heartfelt prayers on real-life topics, journaling prompts, and encouraging meditations that you can use as a helpful resource in your quiet time with God.

Anger

Dear God,

I am so angry I am about to explode! But You already know that. In fact, You know the situation that has triggered these feelings even better than I do.

Is it okay for a Christian to be angry? It can't be right for me to injure others with harsh words and sharp tones when Jesus told us to "turn the other cheek." But what am I supposed to do with these powerful emotions? Please show me how to deal with this anger in a way that pleases You.

In Jesus' name,
Amen.

Hot tempers start fights;
a calm, cool spirit keeps the peace.

PROVERBS 15:18 MSG

A fool gives full vent to anger,
but the wise quietly holds it back.

PROVERBS 29:11 NRSV

When you are angry, do not sin. And do not go on being
angry all day. Do not give the devil a way to defeat you.

EPHESIANS 4:26–27 ICB

Human anger does not achieve God's righteous purpose.

JAMES 1:20 GNT

He who is slow to anger is better than the mighty,
And he who rules his spirit than he who takes a city.

PROVERBS 16:32 NKJV

Don't ever forget that it is best to listen much, speak little,
and not become angry.

JAMES 1:19 TLB

When a man grows angry, his reason rides out.

THOMAS FULLER

JAYNE WAS A COLLEGE STUDENT WITH AN INABILITY to express the anger and resentment she felt. "My roommate gets to the point sometimes where she just explodes emotionally to let off steam," she said. "I have deep feelings, too, but I'm not sure that a Christian is supposed to let off steam."

How are Christians to behave when they are angry? Paul admonished: "Be angry, and yet do not sin" (Ephesians 4:26 NASB). Anger is a natural human emotion, but the expression of anger can sometimes be unhealthy—which is not how a Christian should act.

Fortunately, the Bible does give us a pattern to follow to deal with our feelings in a more open and honest way. In Psalm 109, David expressed anger and rage against an enemy. But David's words didn't surprise God. God already knew what he was thinking and feeling. David was simply expressing those feelings honestly before his God. The way David acknowledged his feelings is healthy.

While anger is natural, you don't have to be controlled by it. Instead, take your feelings to the Lord. When you are able to "dump" your hurt and hatred before your Heavenly Father, you will be less likely to dump it on your loved ones and family members in a destructive way. In addition, when you allow the Holy Spirit to control your thoughts and actions, you will be surprised at how your life becomes filled with less anger and more love, compassion, and forgiveness.

What situations make you the angriest? How can you begin to turn those angry feelings over to the Lord?

_____

_____

_____

_____

_____

_____

_____

_____

_____

_____

_____

_____

_____

_____

Anxiety

Heavenly Father,

I am really struggling with anxiety right now. My mind is bombarded by thoughts of What if this? *and* What about that? *It is affecting my ability to think clearly and robbing me of the peace that I know You desire me to have.*

Jesus is the Prince of Peace, and I need Him to be that to me now. Lead me to scriptures that will reassure my troubled heart and calm my fears. Help me to solidly place my trust in You so that anxiety can find no home in me.

In Jesus' name,
Amen.

Anxiety in a man's heart weighs it down,
But a good word makes it glad.

PROVERBS 12:25 NASB

Banish anxiety from your heart
and cast off the troubles of your body.

ECCLESIASTES 11:10 NIV

When anxiety was great within me,
your consolation brought joy to my soul.

PSALM 94:19 NIV

Cast all your anxiety on him because he cares for you.

1 PETER 5:7 NIV

May God bless you richly and grant you increasing free-
dom from all anxiety and fear.

1 PETER 1:2 TLB

I am filled with trouble and anxiety,
but your commandments bring me joy.

PSALM 119:143 GNT

*The beginning of anxiety is the end of faith, and the beginning
of true faith is the end of anxiety.*

GEORGE MULLER

IN OUR FRANTIC, STRESS-FILLED SOCIETY, a great deal of money is spent on a "cure" for anxiety. People do many things to try to find peace: consume alcohol, take illegal drugs, turn to the refrigerator, even mindlessly repeat mantras that have no real meaning—all to reduce their anxiety. One lady said, "Whenever I feel anxious, I go on a shopping spree!" Prescription drugs are regularly dispensed to try to bring calm to stressed-out people.

God doesn't want us to be consumed by anxiety! But there is a better way to cope with stress and anxiety than the strategies the world has to offer. The Bible tells us that we are to cast our cares upon Jesus, because He cares for us. (See 1 Peter 5:7 NKJV.) Jesus is the answer for our chaos and turmoil. He is our peace in the midst of a busy and stress-filled world.

We all desperately need the peace of God to soothe our anxious spirits. The Bible tells us: "Be anxious for nothing, but in everything by prayer and supplication, with thanksgiving, let your requests be made known to God; and the peace of God, which surpasses all understanding, will guard your hearts and minds through Christ Jesus" (Philippians 4:6–7 NKJV). When we take our worries to the Lord in prayer, and then leave them at His feet, we will receive peace and comfort like we have never known before.

Are you "anxious for nothing"? If not, begin to cast your cares upon Jesus. Bring Him all of your concerns, worries, and fears, and let Him give you His amazing peace in return.

What cares do you need to cast onto Jesus today?

_____

_____

_____

_____

_____

_____

_____

_____

_____

_____

_____

_____

_____

_____

_____

_____

Depression

Heavenly Father,

I hate it when I feel like this. It is as though a gloomy cloud has enveloped me, and it seems like I'm climbing uphill with weights on. Everything takes so much effort that it hardly seems worth it. I feel numb inside and I don't know how to shake it.

I turn to You, Father, for comfort and strength. As I lean on Your everlasting arms, fill me with Your peace. Let the healing balm of Your Spirit wash over me and restore to me the joy of my salvation.

In Jesus' name,
Amen.

The eternal God is your refuge,
and underneath are the everlasting arms.

DEUTERONOMY 33:27 NIV

"I called to the LORD in my distress,
and he answered me.
From the depths of my watery grave I cried for help,
and you heard my cry."

JONAH 2:2 GWT

I am standing here depressed and gloomy,
but I will meditate upon your kindness to this lovely land.
. . . O my soul, don't be discouraged. Don't be upset.
Expect God to act! For I know that I shall again have
plenty of reason to praise him for all that he will do.
He is my help! He is my God!

PSALM 42:6, 11 TLB

He will not break the bruised reed,
nor quench the dimly burning flame.
He will encourage the fainthearted,
those tempted to despair.

ISAIAH 42:3 TLB

JESUS UNDERSTANDS LIKE NO ONE ELSE. He will lead you through the darkness and into the light. Everybody feels depressed at times. It doesn't mean that you're bad or a loser. It just means that the struggles of life have knocked you down so far that you don't know how to get back up.

You definitely don't need a to-do list. But the following tips may help:

- Sometimes, depression stems from anger concerning a situation. Ask the Lord to show you if this is the case. If so, you may need to write a letter to someone express-ing your anger and then never mail it. This exercise re-moves the anger from you and allows your true feelings to surface.

- It may be useful to see a professional to help you sort through your feelings. There are many great Christian counselors. Seeing a counselor is like going to a mechanic when your car has a problem. It just makes sense!

- Spend time reading God's Word. Choose an easy-to-read translation and just read until you feel like stopping. The book of Psalms is a great place to begin because it records many of David's struggles and sor-rows. The Bible is supernatural and will bring healing and peace to you.

- Play uplifting Christian music in your home. When Saul was disturbed, David played a harp to soothe him (1 Samuel 16:23). Good music will touch your heart and soul.

- If you need a good cry—then give yourself permission. It releases much pent-up emotion.

- Share your pain with trusted friends and ask them for their prayers. Then heed their godly advice. Remember, they love you and want to help.

Turn to the Lord. Don't run from Him. He loves you and wants to heal your broken heart.

Don't give up!

Write down one promise from God's Word on a note card. Carry it with you today and refer to it often.

# Disappointment

God,

I am so disappointed. I had such high hopes only to have them dashed. Now I feel hurt and angry, and my faith is being sorely tested. I know it's not Your fault, but why didn't You do something?

Forgive me, Father. That line of thinking will only drag me down. I know that You are utterly trustworthy. Comfort my heart and use this situation to teach me and help me to grow. At least then something good will come from it. I know You love me, Father, and I put my trust in You.

In Your Son's name,
Amen.

Do not let your heart envy sinners,
but always continue in the fear of the LORD.
Surely there is a future,
and your hope will not be cut off.

PROVERBS 23:17–18 NRSV

The Lord looks after those who fear him,
those who put their hope in his love.

PSALM 33:18 NCV

Trust in Him at all times, you people;
Pour out your heart before Him;
God is a refuge for us.

PSALM 62:8 NKJV

Unrelenting disappointment leaves you heartsick,
but a sudden good break can turn life around.

PROVERBS 13:12 MSG

Stay with GOD!
Take heart. Don't quit.

PSALM 27:14 MSG

*Never forget: God is a God of miracles. He can turn even the
biggest disappointments into something beautiful.*

EVER BEEN DISAPPOINTED?

Everyone has, but it doesn't make it any easier. Disappointments come in all shapes and sizes. Those gorgeous shoes you wanted weren't available in your size. Okay, you can live with that. But what about when you don't get the promotion you deserve and have been striving for? That is much harder, isn't it?

Facing and dealing with disappointment can be tricky. Although the small ones seem unworthy of notice, when they are repeated many times over, you can begin to build a wall around yourself for protection. You begin to stifle any excitement you have about things you are hoping for. You begin to harden yourself to the joy you would normally have in anticipation of certain things. In fact, if you have enough disappointments, you may never let yourself dream again. You may think, *What's the use—nothing good ever happens to me. I'm not going to even try anymore!*

This may sound a little extreme to you. You may just be fighting a few small discouragements. But beware—make sure you deal with each setback individually. If you feel hurt or angry about a recent letdown, admit it to yourself instead of stuffing your feelings. Take your discouragement to the Lord. He understands your every feeling and wants to help you. You may also need to examine your expectations—unmet expectations cause turmoil. And if your expectations were unrealistic, you may need to make an adjustment in your thinking.

Disappointments are going to come. But don't let them ruin your life. Dare to dream again. God is the One who makes dreams come true, and He wants to do that for you!

Are you dealing with a disappointment right now? Have you turned it over to the Lord?

_____

_____

_____

_____

_____

_____

_____

_____

_____

_____

_____

Failure

God,

I do not think I have ever felt so low. This failure has knocked the wind out of me. Help me catch my breath! Right now I cannot see past this thing, and I wonder if I will ever recover. How will I ever find the courage to try again?

I turn to You, Father, because You are my only hope. Even though I have failed, You never will. Help me to learn from this defeat, so I will not repeat my mistakes. Lead me to the path of success You have planned for me.

In Jesus' name,
Amen.

We know that in all things
God works for the good of those who love him,
who have been called according to his purpose.

ROMANS 8:28 NIV

Enemy, don't laugh at me.
I have fallen, but I will get up again.
I sit in the shadow of trouble now,
but the Lord will be a light for me.

MICAH 7:8 NCV

[Jesus said,] "I have prayed for you,
that your faith may not fail."

LUKE 22:32 NASB

We are perplexed because we don't know
why things happen as they do, but we don't give up
and quit. . . . We get knocked down, but we get up again
and keep going.

2 CORINTHIANS 4:8–9 TLB

God gives a hand to those down on their luck,
gives a fresh start to those ready to quit.

PSALM 145:14 MSG

The secret of success is constancy to purpose.
BENJAMIN DISRAELI

HAVE YOU EVER TRIED TO DO SOMETHING, BUT FAILED? Everyone has. And it's all right because you can learn a lot of lessons from failure. Maybe a change needs to take place before you try again, or maybe this failure is only a temporary setback. These are healthy perspectives to consider when you fail.

But the unhealthy way to deal with a defeat is to translate the event into the wrong assumption that you are a failure. When you look at the failure as an isolated event, you are able to be more objective and to find solutions. But when you take it personally and begin to attack yourself, you're setting yourself up for discouragement and more failure. This kind of thinking doesn't help you; it cripples you and makes you fearful of trying again.

Abraham Lincoln is a great example of someone who didn't let failure deter him. In an amazing sequence of events, he was defeated in a run for the state legislature, he failed in a business venture, he lost in his attempt to be House Speaker, he failed in his run for the Senate twice, and then he even lost the nomination for vice president. However, the next thing he tried was a success. He ran for president. And the rest, as they say, is history!

Lincoln was not extraordinary. He was just an ordinary man who didn't quit. When he failed, he got back up and tried again. And you can too! If you've had a recent bungle, tell yourself the truth. You failed—but you're not a failure! Give the Lord your disappointment and then seek His wisdom for your next step. Your next attempt may lead to great success!

Have you recently failed at something? What steps can you take so you will succeed next time?

_____

_____

_____

_____

_____

_____

_____

_____

_____

_____

_____

_____

_____

Fear

Heavenly Father,

Fear is knocking at the door of my heart, trying to overtake me, and I need Your help to conquer it. Your Word says that You have not given me the spirit of fear, but of power, love, and a sound mind. Therefore, I resist fear.

Since things always seem worse in the dark, I ask You to shine Your light on this situation so I can see it from Your perspective. Thank You for Your promise to never leave nor forsake me. With You by my side, I can face—and overcome—every fear.

In Jesus' name,
Amen.

"Fear not, for I am with you;
Be not dismayed, for I am your God.
I will strengthen you,
Yes, I will help you,
I will uphold you with My righteous right hand."

ISAIAH 41:10 NKJV

The Lord himself will go before you.
He will be with you. He will not leave you or forget you.
Don't be afraid. Don't worry.

DEUTERONOMY 31:8 ICB

"I am the LORD, your God,
who takes hold of your right hand
and says to you, Do not fear;
I will help you."

ISAIAH 41:13 NIV

Say to those who are of a fearful heart,
"Be strong, do not fear!
Here is your God. . . .
He will come and save you."

ISAIAH 35:4 NRSV

There is nothing to fear when Jesus is near.

WHEN YOU WERE A KID, WERE YOU EVER AFRAID that there might be monsters under your bed? It was the fear of the unknown. As children, we don't have the reasoning capabilities or the experience necessary to know that there really are no such things as monsters. Our perspective is limited. We need someone with more experience and insight to assure us that monsters don't exist. When a parent says we'll be okay and not to worry, we believe them. Why? Because we know they love us, and we know they wouldn't lie.

As we mature, we still have fears of the unknown. What will happen if I get laid off? What if I can't make new friends when I move? Worries like this plague our minds and hearts. They can actually paralyze us and keep us from taking risks in life. Wouldn't it be great if we knew someone who had gone before and could tell us that everything will be all right? Well, we do. There is a quote that says it all: Don't be afraid of tomorrow; for God is already there. (Author Unknown)

God has the distinct advantage of being omniscient— He knows everything! He has gone before, and He knows the future and how everything is going to shake out. And best of all, He loves you. So, just like the parent who tucked you in and told you that no monster was going to get you, God can give you His assurance that all will work out for your good. In fact, He can make it happen! Why not tell Him your fears and let Him give you His peace and assurance?

What is your greatest fear right now? Ask God to give you a promise from His Word concerning your situation.

_____

_____

_____

_____

_____

_____

_____

_____

_____

_____

_____

_____

Grief

Father God,

My heart is agonizing over this loss. In fact, grief has so consumed me that I wonder if I will ever experience joy and laughter again. Everything in me wants to run from this pain, to do something— anything—so that I won't feel it anymore, but I know that lasting comfort can be found only in You. Anything else will provide only temporary relief and prolong the healing process.

I run to You, Father. Hold me in Your loving, compassionate, healing embrace. Guide my journey to restoration that I may smile again.

In the name of Your Son,
Amen.

Blessed are they that mourn:
for they shall be comforted.

MATTHEW 5:4 KJV

The ransomed of the LORD shall return,
and come to Zion with singing;
everlasting joy shall be upon their heads;
they shall obtain joy and gladness,
and sorrow and sighing shall flee away.

ISAIAH 35:10 NRSV

You changed my sorrow into dancing.
You took away my clothes of sadness,
and clothed me in happiness.

PSALM 30:11 NCV

The LORD is near to the brokenhearted,
and saves the crushed in spirit.

PSALM 34:18 NRSV

[Jesus said,] "I tell you the truth, you will weep and
mourn. . . . You will grieve, but your grief will turn to joy."

JOHN 16:20 NIV

Loss brings pain, but God brings comfort.

WE ALL EXPERIENCE GRIEF at one time or another. We may experience the loss of a job or a friendship, a divorce, or the death of a loved one. In times like this, we hurt and need comfort. So where do we find that comfort?

First and foremost, in God. This may sound trite when you feel that your world has just collapsed, but the Bible says that God is the source of all comfort. (See 2 Corinthians 1:3.) God loves you, and He is the only One who truly feels and understands the pain you feel. He longs to fill you with His peace and hope.

Sometimes we may blame Him for our situation or we may just think He doesn't care. But don't let your grief deceive you. God is good, and all good things come from Him. He does not enjoy seeing you suffer. Go to Him, pour out your troubles, and allow Him to heal your broken heart.

The second place to find comfort is from friends. Not acquaintances, in this instance, but "true-blue" friends. Since this is a very vulnerable time for you, choose these people carefully. And don't be ashamed to call them when you need to talk. Most friends want to help but don't know how. If you give them some concrete ways to help, you'll find them more than willing.

The third place to find comfort may surprise you. This

person should be your strongest ally. That person is you. Only you know the full extent of the loss you feel. So, why not give yourself some comfort? Allow yourself some down time to just do something you love, like watching a funny movie or taking a bubble bath. Be patient with yourself and treat yourself with the tender loving care that you deserve and need at this time.

Grief packs a powerful wallop; but with God, your friends, and you on your side, you will make it.

Make a short list of some things you can do for yourself to feel comforted and loved.

_____

_____

_____

_____

_____

_____

_____

_____

_____

_____

Loneliness

Dear Lord,

*I feel lonely and sad. I don't feel like
I belong anywhere or to anyone. Please
wrap Your loving arms around me and
show me that You are with me.*

*Help me to know that You will never,
ever leave me, no matter what. Open my
eyes to see that You are with me right now,
in this very moment. Thank You, Lord,
that You have heard my cry.*

In Jesus' name,
Amen.

I have set the LORD continually before me;
Because He is at my right hand, I will not be shaken.

PSALM 16:8 NASB

You will make known to me the path of life;
In Your presence is fullness of joy;
In Your right hand there are pleasures forever.

PSALM 16:11 NASB

Turn to me and be gracious to me,
for I am lonely and afflicted.

PSALM 25:16 NASB

I will rejoice and be glad in Your lovingkindness,
Because You have seen my affliction;
You have known the troubles of my soul.

PSALM 31:7 NASB

Many are the afflictions of the righteous,
But the LORD delivers him out of them all.

PSALM 34:19 NASB

When you feel alone, God is only a prayer away.

LONELINESS. Even the word sounds sad, doesn't it? It's the universal feeling that no one wants to feel. Instead, we want to know that we are significant and that our lives matter to someone. We want someone to understand us, care about us, and know us inside and out.

It is understandable that we would feel this way because God has created each one of us with a deep desire to be connected. And there is nothing wrong with that desire as long as we turn to the right source to meet that need. So, where do we turn when we are overwhelmed with that sense of loneliness? The real solution comes only when we turn to God. He is the only One who understands us and knows us fully. He is absolutely crazy about us! Can you believe that? Well, it is true. The Bible says that He is intimately acquainted with all our ways. (See Psalm 139:3 NASB.) It also says that He thinks about us all the time. (See Psalm 139:17 NASB.) That is amazing, and it is also comforting.

So, if you are feeling lonely and like nobody cares about you, take comfort in these words. "I am convinced that nothing can ever separate us from his love . . . Our fears for today, our worries about tomorrow, and even the powers of hell can't keep God's love away" (Romans 8:38 NLT). Take a moment and imagine yourself as a little child crawling up into the Father's lap. He is waiting for you, right now, with His arms outstretched. He longs to hold you and comfort you. He wants you to know—you are not alone.

Imagine yourself in the arms of your Heavenly Father—what is He saying to you?

Rejection

Heavenly Father,

The sting of rejection has cut me to my core. One minute I am reeling in pain; the next I am filled with rage and want to retaliate. I feel so worthless! Maybe I deserve to be rejected.

But then I remember that Jesus knows exactly how rejection feels. And I can't be worthless if He chose to pay such a high price for me. Thank You, Father, that You will never reject me. Hold me in Your arms as I drink in Your healing love and acceptance. Help me to forgive as Jesus did.

In His name,
Amen.

Do not reject me or forsake me,
O God my Savior.
Though my father and mother forsake me,
the LORD will receive me.

PSALM 27:9–10 NIV

The LORD will not reject his people;
he will never forsake his inheritance.

PSALM 94:14 NIV

For the sake of his great name the LORD
will not reject his people, because the LORD was pleased
to make you his own.

1 SAMUEL 12:22 NIV

[Jesus said,] "Those the Father has given me will come to
me, and I will never reject them."

JOHN 6:37 NLT

[Jesus said,] "He who listens to you listens to me;
he who rejects you rejects me;
but he who rejects me rejects him who sent me."

LUKE 10:16 NIV

*Not only has Jesus experienced rejection as you have, but He
alone can heal you of its pain.*

EVERYONE KNOWS WHAT IT FEELS LIKE TO BE CRITICIZED AND REJECTED, often by the very people whom we desperately want to please the most. At some point in our lives, we all have been ignored, overlooked, or rejected by parents, teachers, and friends.

Although other people may reject us, God never will. The acceptance of God is not based on who we are or what we can do—instead, it is based entirely on His kindness and mercy: "But when the kindness of God our Savior and His love for mankind appeared, He saved us, not on the basis of deeds which we have done in righteousness, but according to His mercy" (Titus 3:4–5 NASB).

It's easy to get defensive when it seems that other people are turning their backs on us. Our human nature wants to impress others, to show them how "good" we are, how talented or wealthy or even how spiritual we can be. But the good news is that God doesn't view us from a "human" perspective. He views us instead through the shed blood of His Son, Jesus.

Rather than rejecting you, Jesus accepts you—just as you are! "Therefore, accept one another, just as Christ also accepted us to the glory of God" (Romans 15:7 NASB). There is no need to perform or pretend, to impress Him by your actions, in order to win His approval. He already loves you—and He proved it by His death for you on the cross.

If you are feeling left out or left behind, remember that Jesus knows how you feel—and He cares. Jesus was "despised and rejected of men," as well (Isaiah 53:3 KJV), and He longs to put His arms of comfort and acceptance around you today.

How can you demonstrate God's love and acceptance to someone else today?

_____

_____

_____

_____

_____

_____

_____

_____

_____

_____

_____

_____

Self-pity

Heavenly Father,

Not that it is any surprise to You, but I've been having a pity party rehearsing all of my failures, disappointments, and hurts. I am thankful that You always listen when I need to unburden my heart, but I have taken it too far, wallowing in "poor, pitiful me."

Enough is enough! Instead of meditating on the negative things in my life, I choose to thank You for all of my blessings. I choose to let go of those who have hurt me, as well as the pain they have caused. I rejoice in You!

In Jesus' name,
Amen.

Why are you down in the dumps, dear soul?
Why are you crying the blues?
Fix my eyes on God—
soon I'll be praising again.
He puts a smile on my face.
He's my God.
When my soul is in the dumps, I rehearse
everything I know of you.

PSALM 42:5–6 MSG

Rejoice always; pray without ceasing; in everything give
thanks; for this is God's will for you in Christ Jesus.

1 THESSALONIANS 5:16–18 NASB

Is your life full of difficulties and temptations?
Then be happy, for when the way is rough,
your patience has a chance to grow.

JAMES 1:2–3 TLB

Fix your thoughts on what is true and good and right.
Think about things that are pure and lovely, and
dwell on the fine, good things in others.
Think about all you can praise God for.

PHILIPPIANS 4:8 TLB

Everyone thinks his sack heaviest.

GEORGE HERBERT

YOU KNOW THE SYMPTOMS—the feelings of "Poor me. Nobody else faces the problems I face." The inner sense that you are alone in your troubles, that no one else in the history of the world has ever had the struggles you are having. Although everyone indulges in self-pity once in a while, it is destructive to our relationship with God and with others—as well as to the plans God has for us. Helen Keller, well-known deaf and blind American author and speaker, once said, "Self-pity is our worst enemy, and if we yield to it, we can never do anything good in the world."

Self-pity isn't God's way. He instructs us to walk in love, which is "not self-seeking," and which "keeps no record of wrongs" (1 Corinthians 13:5 NIV). A good antidote for self-pity is forgiveness. As we forgive those who offend us, we can let go of our negative emotions and receive the comfort and healing that can come only from God.

Another good antidote for self-pity is thankfulness. The Bible says: "Thank [God] in everything [no matter what the circumstances may be, be thankful and give thanks], for this is the will of God for you [who are] in Christ Jesus" (1 Thessalonians 5:18 AMP). No matter what is going on in our lives, we always have reason to give thanks to God and praise Him.

You have been chosen by God, not just to live eternally

with Him in heaven, but to make a difference for Him while you're still here on earth. Don't allow self-pity to neutralize all the good you can do in this world.

Do you indulge in self-pity, or do you practice the love and forgiveness of God each day?

Stress

Dear Lord,

Please help me. I am so stressed and feel as if I am spinning out of control. There are circumstances in my life that I cannot change, and I am overwhelmed.

Lord, help me to put everything down and come and sit in Your presence. I relinquish control of my burdens. Cover me in Your peace and love. I give to You this tangled mess of worries and know that You will deliver me.

In Jesus' name,
Amen.

Cast thy burden upon the LORD, and he shall sustain thee:
He shall never suffer the righteous to be moved.

PSALM 55:22 KJV

Jesus said, "Come to me, all of you who are weary and
carry heavy burdens, and I will give you rest."

MATTHEW 11:28 NLT

Our soul waiteth for the LORD:
He is our help and our shield.

PSALM 33:20 KJV

"That's right. Because I, your GOD,
have a firm grip on you and I'm not letting go.
I'm telling you, 'Don't panic.
I'm right here to help you.'"

ISAIAH 41:13 MSG

Don't fret or worry. Instead of worrying, pray.
Let petitions and praises shape your worries into prayers,
letting God know your concerns.

PHILIPPIANS 4:6 MSG

Worrying isn't constructive;
praying to the One with the answers is.

ARE YOU STRESSING OVER LIFE?
Do you lie down at night and just stare at the ceiling because you're so bothered? Do you forget the one thing you went into the store to purchase, but come out with ten other things? Well, hundreds of thousands of people are in the same boat!

The world is on a never-ending merry-go-round of activity—to get, achieve, and acquire. However, God wants us to have higher priorities and trust Him to take care of all the rest. We are on a different mission—we are here to know and enjoy Him, and then show His goodness to others.

How can we do that when our lives are so harried and frazzled? It may mean slowing down and saying no, even to good activities, so that you can experience God's best in your life. It also could mean taking inventory of your life and establishing new priorities for how you and your family spend your waking hours. It could even mean learning to experience "Sabbath rest"—no, not a Sunday church ritual—but a deliberate coming away from all the hustle and bustle, to reflect, renew, and recharge.

God knew we would face tremendous pressures in our world today, but He also promised us the grace needed to live in this hectic, nonstop world. He loves us and desires that we experience the abundant life that He promised we could have. It is only when we follow His priorities that we will see the undue stress leave our lives.

When was the last time you took the time to meet God for real fellowship over a good cup of coffee? He's waiting now . . . for you!

What are some things that you could let go so that you can experience less stress?

_____

_____

_____

_____

_____

_____

_____

_____

_____

_____

_____

_____

_____

Temptation

Heavenly Father,

*Temptation is knocking on my door,
and everything in me wants to give in.
I don't want to fall into this trap, but I
need Your help.*

*Thank You for Your promise that as I
submit myself to You and resist the devil,
he will flee from me. Cause me to see this
trick for what it is so it will lose its appeal
and give me wisdom so I can avoid future
temptations.*

*I cannot overcome this situation
alone, but because Christ lives in me and
strengthens me, I will triumph.*

*In Jesus' name,
Amen.*

The temptations that come into you life are no different from what others experience. And God is faithful. He will keep the temptation from becoming so strong that you can't stand up against it. When you are tempted, he will show you a way out so that you will not give in to it.

1 Corinthians 10:13 nlt

Give yourselves completely to God.
Stand against the devil, and the devil will run from you.

James 4:7 ncv

Since he himself has now been through suffering and temptation, he knows what it is like when we suffer and are tempted, and he is wonderfully able to help us.

Hebrews 2:18 tlb

We are not ignorant about Satan's scheming.

2 Corinthians 2:11 gwt

Put on all the armor that God supplies. In this way you can take a stand against the devil's strategies.

Ephesians 6:11 gwt

'Tis one thing to be tempted . . . , another thing to fall.
William Shakespeare

WHAT IS TEMPTATION? Something we desire that is wrong. And it has its roots in Adam and Eve's experience in the Garden of Eden. God commanded them not to eat from a certain tree, or the consequence would be death. (See Genesis 2:17.)

Just to be clear, there were other trees to eat from, so provision was not an issue. The issue was obedience—God gave them specific instructions. Ignorance wasn't an issue either; they clearly understood what God expected of them.

Then came temptation. The devil, disguised as a snake, approached Eve and convinced her that God really didn't mean what He said—surely she wouldn't die if she ate from the tree. He also convinced her that the fruit from the tree would open her eyes and that she would be like God. Eve believed his lies, and we've been tempted ever since. (See Genesis 3:1–7.)

Isn't it interesting that Satan's method of temptation has not changed? His strategy is the same: convince his "victims" that there will be no lasting consequences to their disobedience and that they will gain something from their actions.

Therefore, it's important to arm ourselves against temptation before temptation comes. Here's how:

- Don't put yourself in a situation where you know you will be tempted.
- Tell yourself the truth. God isn't in the business of deprivation. He loves you and wants your best. He isn't withholding from you. (See James 1:17.)
- Ask God to deliver you from temptation daily.
- Pray that God will give you a willing and obedient heart.

Begin to apply these principles today. God wants you to overcome temptation.

What temptation are you dealing with now? What principle can you apply to help you overcome?

_____

_____

_____

_____

_____

_____

_____

_____

Acceptance

Father God,

Sometimes I feel like a square peg in a round hole. People mean well, but so often their acceptance is conditional. I am tired of jumping through hoops and trying to please others. Besides, some people won't accept me regardless of what I do, and that hurts.

What a relief it is to know that Your acceptance is not based on anything I do or do not do. You accept me because of who You are. I am so thankful that You will never reject me. With You I am free to be me.

In Jesus' name,
Amen.

With everlasting love I will have compassion on you,
says the LORD, your Redeemer.

ISAIAH 54:8 NRSV

"I have loved you with an everlasting love;
Therefore I have drawn you with lovingkindness."

JEREMIAH 31:3 NASB

You are my servant;
I have chosen you and have not rejected you.

ISAIAH 41:9 NIV

For the sake of his great name the LORD will not reject his
people, because the LORD was pleased to make you his own.

1 SAMUEL 12:22 NIV

He made us accepted in the Beloved.

EPHESIANS 1:6 NKJV

[Jesus said,] "The Father gives me my people. Every one of
them will come to me, and I will always accept them."

JOHN 6:37 NCV

*There is nothing you could ever do that would change God's
love for you. You're the apple of His eye, and
He's crazy about you!*

WE ALL NEED TO BE ACCEPTED AND LOVED. We long for someone to think we're the "best thing since sliced bread." In fact, this need is so strong that it can drive us to do many foolish things. Just ask any teenager swayed by peer pressure.

But since God promises to meet every need, this need for acceptance is no exception. God longs to be the One to whom you look for affirmation. Since He created you, He is well acquainted with everything about you. And the amazing thing is that He loves you and will never change His opinion of you, regardless of any of your actions. That may sound too good to be true, but it is true. God has already made up His mind about you.

But we tend to be suspicious of this "no-strings attached" type of love because we are used to conditional love—the kind of love that says, "I will love you as long as you do this," or "I will not love you if you do this." But God's love is different. It is not a reflection of how lovable we are—but how loving He is! The Bible says that God is love (1 John 4:8), so when He shows you that love, He is merely expressing His own nature. You can trust Him. When He says He loves you, it is not a passing fancy that will change with the tide. Because He never changes—He is always the same.

And He always accepts you—no matter what! He is on your side and will never give up on you. Choose to believe it—because it's true!

What is keeping you from accepting God's opinion of you?

_____

_____

_____

_____

_____

_____

_____

_____

_____

_____

_____

_____

_____

_____

Contentment

Father in Heaven,

I feel so restless inside, so dissatisfied. An insatiable desire for more consumes me, yet no matter how much I attain, contentment evades my grasp. Deep inside I know this is not right and that it does not please You. Forgive me, Father, and show me Your way.

Your Word says that You are the God of peace, and I ask You to settle my striving heart with heavenly contentment. Thank You for all the good things You have given me, and I choose today to be thankful and content in You.

In Jesus' name,
Amen.

There is great gain in godliness combined
with contentment.

1 TIMOTHY 6:6 NRSV

I say it is better to be content
with what little you have.
Otherwise, you will always be struggling for more,
and that is like chasing the wind.

ECCLESIASTES 4:6 NCV

As for me, my contentment is not in wealth but
in seeing you and knowing all is well between us.
And when I awake in heaven, I will be fully satisfied,
for I will see you face to face.

PSALM 17:15 TLB

Because your love is better than life,
I will praise you. . . .
I will be content as if I had eaten the best foods.

PSALM 63:3, 5 NCV

Keep your lives free from the love of money and
be content with what you have.

HEBREWS 13:5 NIV

*He is richest who is content with the least,
for content is the wealth of nature.*

SOCRATES

WHEN WAS THE LAST TIME you met someone who was truly contented with what they had in life? Someone who wasn't striving to be more, to do more, to acquire more? This sort of person is becoming extremely rare in our culture, but the Bible tells us that we should learn to be satisfied with what we have, no matter in what state we find ourselves in life. (See Philippians 4:11–12.)

According to a 2001 study conducted by the American Psychological Association, people who consider themselves to be "contented" also have good self-esteem and the ability to see positive things in their lives. They have a good network of friends and at least a few close ones with whom they can share intimate details. They also consider their faith to be one of the most important influences in their lives.

When you make the decision to be satisfied with whatever God provides, you will find that there is little that can ruffle your feathers. So what if you didn't get the bonus you were hoping for? God has provided you with food and shelter. So what if you aren't married by the time you thought you would be? God has provided you with wonderful friends—and He will bring you a mate in His perfect timing. So what if the husband you have been blessed with doesn't live up to your every expectation? You can focus on his good qualities and leave the rest to God.

Contentment helps you focus on what you do have instead of what you don't—and life becomes a whole lot sweeter in the process.

What do you have to be thankful for?

_____

_____

_____

_____

_____

_____

_____

_____

_____

_____

_____

_____

_____

_____

_____

Endurance

Father God,

I am struggling to hang on. It has been like this for so long, and I have grown weary. Sometimes I do not know if I can take another step.

But then I remember—I am not alone, and it is not all up to me. You are the strength of my life. The same Spirit that raised Christ from the dead dwells in me! As I wait upon You, Father, renew my vision and determination. You have sent the Greater One to live in me; therefore, I can and will endure until I win.

In Jesus' name,
Amen.

Those who trust in the LORD are like Mount Zion,
which cannot be shaken but endures forever.

PSALM 125:1 NIV

Everything that was written in the past was
written to teach us, so that through endurance and the
encouragement of the Scriptures we might have hope.

ROMANS 15:4 NIV

In our trouble God had comforted us—and this, too, to
help you: to show you from our personal experience how
God will tenderly comfort you when you undergo these
same sufferings. He will give you the strength to endure.

2 CORINTHIANS 1:6–7 TLB

His glorious power will make you patient and strong
enough to endure anything, and you will be truly happy.

COLOSSIANS 1:11 CEV

You must learn to endure everything, so that you will be
completely mature and not lacking in anything.

JAMES 1:4 CEV

When you get to the end of your rope, tie a knot and hang on.

FRANKLIN D. ROOSEVELT

DURING A COMMUTER FLIGHT from Portland, Maine, to Boston several years ago, the pilot, Henry Dempsey, heard an unusual noise near the rear of the small aircraft. He turned the controls over to his copilot and went back to investigate.

As he reached the tail section, the plane hit an air pocket, and Dempsey was tossed against the rear door. He quickly discovered the source of the mysterious noise. The rear door had not been properly latched prior to takeoff, and it flew open. He was instantly sucked out of the jet.

The copilot, seeing the red light that indicated an open door, radioed the nearest airport, requesting permission to make an emergency landing. He reported that the pilot had fallen out of the plane, and he requested a helicopter search of that area of the ocean.

After the plane landed, they found Henry Dempsey— holding on to the outdoor ladder of the aircraft. Somehow he had caught the ladder, held on for ten minutes as the plane flew 200 mph at an altitude of 4,000 feet, and then, at landing, kept his head from hitting the runway. It took airport personnel several minutes to pry Dempsey's fingers from the ladder.

Things in life may feel turbulent, and you may not feel like holding on. But, like Henry Dempsey, have you considered the alternative? Sometimes all you can do is hold on as tightly as you can and try to enjoy the ride!

Hebrews 10:36 says, "You have need of endurance, so that after you have done the will of God, you may receive the promise" (NKJV). No matter what you are facing, with God's help you can endure the situation—and receive His amazing promises as a result.

What situations are you currently "enduring"? How does the promise of a future reward help you to persevere?

_____

_____

_____

_____

_____

_____

_____

_____

_____

_____

_____

Forgiveness

Heavenly Father,

I blew it—again. When will I ever learn? Don't You get tired of me asking for forgiveness? I know I desire to live in such a way that I don't need it so often.

Mercifully, You know that I am only human and that despite my best efforts, I sometimes come up short. Thank You for sending Your Son to pay the price for my mistakes and failures. With humility and gratitude, I ask You to forgive me, and I receive Your pardon now. And because You forgive me, I choose to forgive myself.

In Jesus' name,
Amen.

The Lord our God is merciful and forgiving, even though
we have rebelled against him.

DANIEL 9:9 NIV

I forgive you all that you have done, says the Lord GOD.

EZEKIEL 16:63 NRSV

Come now, and let us reason together,
saith the LORD: though your sins be as scarlet,
they shall be as white as snow.

ISAIAH 1:18 KJV

I, even I, am he that blotteth out thy transgressions for
mine own sake, and will not remember thy sins.

ISAIAH 43:25 KJV

They shall all know me, . . . says the LORD; for I will
forgive their iniquity, and remember their sin no more.

JEREMIAH 31:34 NRSV

Thou, Lord, art good, and ready to forgive;
And plenteous in mercy unto all them that call upon thee.

PSALM 86:5 KJV

To err is human; to forgive, divine.

ALEXANDER POPE

THERE IS A STORY OF A LITTLE BOY standing in front of the Washington Monument. "I want to buy it, and I have a quarter," he told the guard. "That's not enough," the guard said. The little boy replied, "I thought you would say that," pulling nine more cents out of his pocket. The guard looked down at the small boy and said, "You need to understand three things. First, thirty-four cents is not enough. Second, the Washington Monument is not for sale. And third, if you are an American citizen, the Washington Monument already belongs to you."

We need to understand the same three things about God's forgiveness: We will never be good enough to deserve it, it is not for sale, and we cannot earn it. But if we have a personal relationship with God, forgiveness already belongs to us.

If you have sinned and need forgiveness, you need to know that God has already made the way possible for you to receive that forgiveness. When we could not or would not reach out to Him, He reached out to us: "God shows his great love for us in this way: Christ died for us while we were still sinners" (Romans 5:8 NCV).

First John 1:10 reminds us that everyone has sinned: "If we claim we have not sinned, we make [God] out to be a liar" (NIV). But His promise is that if we acknowledge

66

our sin and repent, His forgiveness is available to us: "If we confess our sins, he is faithful and just and will forgive us our sins and purify us from all unrighteousness" (v. 9 NIV).

What an amazing God we have, who offers His forgiveness freely to everyone who asks Him for it! Do you need forgiveness today? Your answer is simple: Forgiveness already belongs to you if you are willing to repent of your sins and confess your need to God. He's waiting!

Thank God for His amazing forgiveness.

God's Favor

Father in Heaven,

To have Your favor is one of the most important things in the world to me. With it comes blessing, favor with people, and open doors. Things just work right when Your favor is present, when You smile upon a person's life. Without Your favor, life is dull and meaningless; potential is limited.

Father, I realize that I don't deserve Your favor, but I humbly ask You to bestow it upon me. Use it to show others how good You are and to draw them unto You. I give You all the glory in advance.

In Jesus' name,
Amen.

Sing praises to the LORD, O you his faithful ones,
and give thanks to his holy name.
For his anger is but for a moment;
his favor is for a lifetime.

PSALM 30:4–5 NRSV

The LORD God is a sun and shield;
the LORD bestows favor and honor;
no good thing does he withhold
from those whose walk is blameless.

PSALM 84:11 NIV

[The Lord said,] "I will look on you with favor and
make you fruitful and increase your numbers,
and I will keep my covenant with you."

LEVITICUS 26:9 NIV

The grace (blessing and favor) of the Lord Jesus Christ (the
Messiah) be with your spirit. Amen (so be it).

PHILEMON 1:25 AMP

*Measure not God's love and favor by your own feeling. The sun
shines as clearly in the darkest day as it does in the brightest.
The difference is not in the sun, but in some clouds.*

RICHARD SIBBES

THIS IS THE YEAR OF THE LORD'S FAVOR! (See Isaiah 61:2; Luke 4:19 NIV.) The Bible declares, boldly in fact, that God wants to shower His favor upon His people: "You, O LORD, will bless the righteous; with favor You will surround him" (Psalm 5:12 NKJV). But many Christians still live their lives with a sense of God's displeasure in the back of their minds: Why would God want to bless me after the way I've lived my life? I need to read my Bible more, go to church more, and pray more before I have earned the favor of God.

Contrary to what many people believe and understand, God's grace is unconditional, and His favor is not dependent on your past behavior. When you accept Jesus into your life, you are forgiven of all of your sins, and you become a child of God—which means that you are immediately qualified for all of the blessings that position entails. In fact, it means that God is actively seeking ways to pour out His favor on you!

If you are wondering if you are worthy of God's blessing, just consider the names the Bible has for you as a child of God: Beloved. Chosen one. Friend of God. Forgiven. Redeemed. Blameless. Holy. Blessed of the Lord. God calls you these names, not because of anything you yourself have done, but because of the names He calls Himself: Faithful. Forgiving. Full of love.

Isn't it time for you to understand and begin to walk in the reality of who you are in God's eyes? You don't have to fear Him or wonder if He wants to bless you. His favor already rests upon you—because you are a daughter of the King!

How can you see God's favor demonstrated in your life?

_____

_____

_____

_____

_____

_____

_____

_____

_____

_____

_____

_____

_____

Guidance

Dear God,

I have a decision to make, but I don't know which way to go. Please guide me so that I will make the right choice. Lead me down the best pathway for my life. Help me to see my situation from Your perspective and keep me from being deceived in any way.

I believe that You want to help me so I am looking to You for an answer. Help me recognize it when it comes.

In Your Son's name,
Amen.

You light my lamp;
The LORD my God illumines my darkness.

PSALM 18:28 NASB

He leads the humble in justice,
And He teaches the humble His way.
All the paths of the LORD are lovingkindness and truth
To those who keep His covenant and His testimonies.

PSALM 25:9–10 NASB

He restores my soul;
He guides me in the paths of righteousness
For His name's sake.

PSALM 23:3 NASB

I will instruct you and teach you
in the way which you should go;
I will counsel you with My eye upon you.

PSALM 32:8 NASB

The path of the righteous is like the light of dawn,
That shines brighter and brighter until the full day.

PROVERBS 4:18 NASB

*Sometimes, the only prerequisite for receiving guidance
is a willingness to receive it.*

SO MANY VOICES—SO MANY PATHS TO CHOOSE. Which way should I go? Here are some simple principles to follow when you're not exactly sure which decision to make:

- Realize that God wants you to know His will in the situation. He does not want you to fail—rather, He longs for you to succeed. Spend time in prayer and in God's Word. This gives God an open door to speak to you and gives you an opportunity to hear when He speaks.

- Get counsel from trusted friends and family. When everyone around you feels you should or should not go in a certain direction—listen and consider—God could be speaking through them.

- Follow peace. When you get quiet and really get honest with yourself, do you feel good about the situation, or do you feel uneasiness? That could be your answer. In the final analysis, God always speaks inside your heart. Jesus said, "My sheep hear My voice, and I know them, and they follow me" (John 10:27 NASB).

- Exercise your faith. When all the lights are green and you really believe this is what you are to do, then go for it! Commit it to God and say, "Lord, I think this is right, so I'm going forward. If for some reason I'm making a mistake, please stop me." And then believe He will. Remember, Jesus is the Good Shepherd.

Prayerfully commit these steps to the Lord and try them. God wants you to make the right choice.

What important decisions do you need guidance in right now?

_____

_____

_____

_____

_____

_____

_____

_____

_____

_____

_____

_____

_____

_____

Healing

Heavenly Father,

Oh, how I need Your healing touch. There is only so much that medical science can do, but You are the Great Physician. When Jesus was here on earth, He was Your representative, and He healed many. Whether it was fever, mental torment, withered limbs, deaf ears, or blind eyes, Jesus never turned anyone away. Thank You that You care about my physical health too. Please make me well today.

In Jesus' name,

Amen.

"I am the LORD who heals you."

EXODUS 15:26 NKJV

Ye shall serve the LORD your God, and he shall bless thy
bread, and thy water; and I will take sickness away from
the midst of thee. There shall nothing cast their young, nor
be barren, in thy land: the number of thy days I will fulfil.

EXODUS 23:25–26 KJV

[The Messiah] was wounded for our transgressions, he was
bruised for our iniquities: the chastisement of our peace
was upon him; and with his stripes we are healed.

ISAIAH 53:5 KJV

Heal me, O LORD, and I shall be healed; save me,
and I shall be saved: for thou art my praise.

JEREMIAH 17:14 KJV

I will restore health unto thee,
And I will heal thee of thy wounds, saith the LORD.

JEREMIAH 30:17 KJV

[The Lord says,] Unto you that fear my name shall the Sun
of righteousness arise with healing in his wings.

MALACHI 4:2 KJV

When you need healing, look to the Great Physician.

ONE DAY AS LISA TUGGED AND PULLED TO REARRANGE THE FURNITURE, she injured her back, ending up with two slipped discs. She went to the doctor, who told her to alternate placing an ice pack and moist heat on her lower back. Even though Lisa followed his directive when she got home, she woke up in the middle of the night with intense pain.

"I could hardly get out of bed, and when I got out, I could hardly walk," Lisa said. The pain was so severe that Lisa eventually decided to read her Bible, hoping to find comfort in its pages. Not knowing what to read for her situation, she selected some Psalms. But she was in such intense pain that she could hardly concentrate.

After reading a few verses, Lisa finally prayed, not for healing exactly, but for relief from the intensity of the pain. Even though there was not an immediate change, she continued to pray night after night as well as continuing the treatment that the doctor had suggested. Little by little, she noticed the pain slowly leaving her back, and eventually it was completely gone.

There is no doubt that God has given wisdom to doctors to help people get well. But He also can touch your body supernaturally. Sometimes, as in Lisa's case, it may be a combination of the two. It's important to note that He is merciful and wants you to be well.

Listen to what God says in Psalm 107:20 NIV about healing: "[The Lord] sent forth his word and healed them; he rescued them from the grave." If you need healing in any part of your being—in your body, mind, or emotions—know that Jesus stands ready to touch you with His strength and power. Why not ask Him?

How have you experienced God's healing touch in your life?

_____

_____

_____

_____

_____

_____

_____

_____

_____

_____

Hope

Father in Heaven,

I am down in the dumps. At times I border on despair because my situation looks so hopeless. Do You see what is happening? Won't You do something?

King David said that he would have fainted if he hadn't believed to see Your goodness in the land of the living. That is where I am now. So many times You have proven Yourself faithful, and I trust that You are moving on my behalf even now. Nothing is impossible with You, the God of miracles. I put my hope in You.

In Jesus' name,
Amen.

May the God of hope fill you with all joy and
peace in believing, so that you will abound in hope by the
power of the Holy Spirit.

ROMANS 15:13 NASB

It is good both to hope and wait quietly
for the salvation of the Lord.

LAMENTATIONS 3:26 TLB

"The LORD is my portion," says my soul,
"Therefore I hope in Him!"
The LORD is good to those who wait for Him,
To the soul who seeks Him.

LAMENTATIONS 3:24–25 NKJV

No one whose hope is in you
will ever be put to shame.

PSALM 25:3 NIV

I will hope continually,
and will praise you yet more and more.
My mouth will tell of your righteous acts.

PSALM 71:14–15 NRSV

Hope means expectancy when things are otherwise hopeless.

G. K. CHESTERTON

DO YOU NEED HOPE TODAY? We all feel that way sometimes. The struggles of everyday living have a way of chipping away at us until we feel beaten down and hopeless.

If that is where you are right now—don't give up! God cares about you and wants to lift your spirit. Psalm 3:3 says, "But You, O LORD, are a shield about me, my glory, and the One who lifts my head" (NASB).

When a person is downcast, he usually walks with his head down. Well, God is in the head-lifting business. He wants to give you hope and encouragement and wants you to walk with your head held high because He is on your side!

Amazingly enough, God links hope to trials and afflictions. In Romans 5: 3–5, we are encouraged to exult in our afflictions knowing that the end result will be hope (NASB). How can that be? Because as we see God move in our behalf over and over again and see Him bring us through trial after trial, we begin to see a pattern. We begin to have a confidence that somehow, some way, God is going to pull us through. It is a confidence born of awareness that there will be progress.

Begin to think back on all your past trials. Think back to all the miraculous things you have seen God do for you over the years. Now, put that confidence into your present situation. Say aloud to yourself right now, "God will see me through! I'm not alone in this." Don't let go of your hope—instead, hold on to it!

List some instances when God brought you through a difficult situation. Why not say thank You to Him for all those times?

_____

_____

_____

_____

_____

_____

_____

_____

_____

_____

_____

_____

_____

_____

Joy

Heavenly Father,

If I let them, my emotions can be like a roller coaster—happy one minute and sad the next—but that kind of instability does not reflect You. I need Your joy—that joy that is the fruit of the Spirit, that is un-moved by circumstances, and that causes others to notice You in my life.

Fill me with the joy of Your presence today. Remind me to rejoice in You when circumstances try to affect my mood. Then cause that joy to spill over onto others to bless them for Your glory.

In Jesus' name,
Amen.

The LORD your God will bless you
in all your harvest and in all the work of your hands,
and your joy will be complete.

DEUTERONOMY 16:15 NIV

The ransomed of the LORD shall return,
And come to Zion with singing,
With everlasting joy on their heads.
They shall obtain joy and gladness;
Sorrow and sighing shall flee away.

ISAIAH 51:11 NKJV

You will go out with joy and be led out in peace.
The mountains and hills will burst into song before you,
and all the trees in the fields will clap their hands.

ISAIAH 55:12 NCV

The joy of the LORD is your strength.

NEHEMIAH 8:10 NASB

I will sing for joy about what your hands have done.

PSALM 92:4 NCV

Happiness is fleeting—joy is lasting.

MANY THINGS IN THIS WORLD PROMISE HAPPINESS, but few ever deliver. Some people think that if they just had more money, they'd be happy. Others think that if they were married (or, if they were single!), or if they could lose weight, or if they had more friends, happiness would fill every day of their lives.

Unlike the world, which is full of empty promises when it comes to happiness, the Bible does not actually promise happiness every day of your life. In fact, being a Christian may actually bring you persecution in this world. But the Bible does promise that no matter what external situations you face in life, you can have joy in everything. And not just a little joy, either. You can "rejoice with joy unspeakable and full of glory" (1 Peter 1:8 KJV).

Joy is much different than happiness. Joseph Marmion once said, "Joy is the echo of God's life within us." Joy comes directly from God, and it is not dependent upon situations in order to be satisfied. With joy, a person can gain or lose great wealth and still find contentment and fulfillment in life. With joy, a person can face bankruptcy, divorce, cancer, even death, and still maintain a positive attitude. Joy does not need a reason. It comes from within, and it is available to you no matter what is going on in your life.

Have you found that your life has become an endless pursuit of happiness—perhaps in a smaller dress size, bigger paycheck, or better relationship? If you are looking toward external things to satisfy you, you will always be disappointed. Maybe it's time to focus on joy instead. It's longer lasting, more reliable, and available today!

What "if only" statements regularly show up in your thoughts? How can you begin to replace them with God's joy?

Patience

Dear God,

I know that patience is a virtue, but I am greatly lacking in it. I get frustrated and impatient so easily. Then I feel guilty because I know that does not reflect Your nature. Not only does impatience have a negative effect on my body and soul, it is sometimes hurtful to others, and that is not acceptable. I want to bless people, not cause them pain.

Father, I need Your help in this area. Strengthen me and remind me to draw on Your patience so that I may respond to life as Jesus did.

In His name,
Amen.

Patient people have great understanding.
PROVERBS 14:29 NCV

I was given mercy so that in me Christ Jesus could show
that he has patience without limit.
1 TIMOTHY 1:16 ICB

Smart people are patient;
they will be honored if they ignore insults.
PROVERBS 19:11 NCV

Farmers do this all the time, waiting for their valuable
crops to mature, patiently letting the rain do its slow
but sure work. Be patient like that.
JAMES 5:7 MSG

We show that we are servants of God by
living a pure life, by our understanding,
by our patience, and by our kindness.
2 CORINTHIANS 6:6 ICB

Patience and encouragement come from God.
ROMANS 15:5 ICB

Patience is the companion of wisdom.
SAINT AUGUSTINE

THE LIGHT TURNS RED JUST AS YOU APPROACH. The older lady in front of you in line at the bank doesn't know how to fill out her deposit slip. Your five-year-old refuses to tie his shoes so that you can leave for school on time.

Every day we are confronted with opportunities to exercise the gift of patience—and some days it is easier to do than others. Perhaps you yourself have recently prayed the famous prayer—"Lord, give me patience—right now!"

But patience isn't something that is given to us overnight. Instead, when the Holy Spirit comes into our lives, He begins to work His fruit as evidence of His presence in our attitudes and behavior. One of those fruits is patience. (See Galatians 5:22 NIV.) As we become filled with more of God's Spirit in our lives, we will find ourselves becoming more patient with the problems and people we encounter every day.

While it may seem difficult or even impossible to display patience in certain situations or even with certain people, it is important to remember that God is always patient with you. *The Message* Bible describes Him as "a God of mercy and grace, endlessly patient—so much love, so deeply true" (Exodus 34:6). In the same way that He chooses to extend His loving grace to you, you can also be "endlessly patient" with those who may require a little bit more of your time and effort.

God has promised that the results of patience are well "worth the wait." The Bible tells us: "A patient man [or woman] has great understanding" (Proverbs 14:29 NIV). Do you need more understanding of a difficult problem? Maybe what you really need is more patience! Ask God to give it to you—in His due time.

What person or situation requires the most patience from you? How can you take a more loving approach?

_____

_____

_____

_____

_____

_____

_____

_____

_____

Peace

Dear Lord,

I need Your peace today. My life is so hectic, and sometimes I feel so frazzled. I get all worked up in my mind worrying over so many things. Help me to turn to You when I feel like everything is coming apart at the seams—including myself!

Fill me with Your peace now as I release all my cares and put my trust in You. And help me, Lord, to walk in Your peace, to make decisions based on peace, and to let Your peace rule my life.

In Your name,
Amen.

Be anxious for nothing, but in everything by prayer
and supplication with thanksgiving let your requests
be made known to God. And the peace of God,
which surpasses all comprehension, will guard your hearts
and your minds in Christ Jesus.

PHILIPPIANS 4:6–7 NASB

[Jesus said,] "Peace I leave with you;
My peace I give to you; not as the world gives
do I give to you. Do not let your heart be troubled,
nor let it be fearful."

JOHN 14:27 NASB

How blessed is the man who finds wisdom. . . .
Her ways are pleasant ways,
And all her paths are peace.

PROVERBS 3:13, 17 NASB

Let the peace of heart which comes from Christ
be always present in your hearts and lives, for this is your
responsibility and privilege as members of his body.

COLOSSIANS 3:15 TLB

Where peace is—anxiety is not.

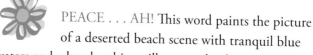 PEACE . . . AH! This word paints the picture of a deserted beach scene with tranquil blue waters and a lonely white sailboat on the distant horizon.

But into this scene comes crashing the word *reality*—hitting the snooze alarm twice, making the mad dash out the door, taking the kids to school late, traffic jams, deadlines, homework, and what will we have for dinner? Is this the "picture" of your life? Sometimes it is hard to have peace on the inside when there is so much turmoil on the outside. But that is exactly what we can have—peace on the inside when there is utter chaos on the outside.

But how? The Bible gives the answer: "In quietness and confidence shall be your strength" (Isaiah 30:15 NKJV). True peace comes when we take the time to sit down with God and allow Him to calm us. We pour out our concerns to Him and wait for His reply. And as He comforts and assures us, we know that all will be okay. We are at peace.

It sounds so simple, doesn't it? The hard part is doing it. So many things compete for our attention. Sometimes, we feel it is impossible. But God would never ask us to do something that we are unable to do. He promises if we put our anxiety aside, turn to Him with our concerns, and thank Him for the answer, that His peace will flood us. That supernatural peace will even guard our minds and hearts.

What a blessing when we are calm and our minds are not whirling with all kinds of anxious thoughts.

Want peace? Jesus said, "Come to Me, all who are weary and heavy-laden, and I will give you rest" (Matthew 11:28 NASB).

List some things that you are anxious about.

_____

_____

_____

_____

_____

_____

_____

_____

_____

_____

_____

_____

Protection

Father God,

This world can be such a scary place. I am thankful I can turn to You for protection. Watch over my comings and goings, and give Your angels charge over me to keep me safe. Deliver me from evil, and with Your presence, cover my home, my property, my vehicle, and everything that pertains to my life.

I am thankful for Your promise that no weapon formed against me will prosper, and I choose to trust You rather than give in to fear. I trust You to protect me in every way.

In Jesus' name,
Amen.

Those who go to God Most High for safety
will be protected by the Almighty.
I will say to the Lord, "You are my place of
safety and protection.
You are my God and I trust you."

PSALM 91:1–2 NCV

The Lord will protect you from all evil. . . .
The Lord will guard your going out and your coming in.

PSALM 121:7–8 NASB

The Lord says, "Whoever loves me, I will save.
I will protect those who know me.
They will call to me, and I will answer them.
I will be with them in trouble;
I will rescue them and honor them."

PSALM 91:14–15 NCV

You are my hiding place;
you will save me from trouble.
I sing aloud of your salvation,
because you protect me.

PSALM 32:7 GNT

Angels are God's celestial security system for His children.

MARIE WATCHED *THE 700 CLUB* FREQUENTLY. Stories were reported of people who had witnessed, firsthand, God's miraculous protection. Marie often wondered if God would do the same for her. She was about to find out!

The day before the event happened, she felt a real uneasiness and began to pray. The next evening, she reluctantly headed out to a Bible study even though she really didn't want to go. As she drove up her street, she passed a house that had several cars parked in and around its driveway. She hit a bump, and a child's Big Wheel rolled out from under her car. She stopped to investigate. Nothing could have prepared her for what she saw. Lying on the road behind her car was a preschool boy! He had ridden the Big Wheel down the driveway between two vehicles and went right underneath her car. The toy sat low to the ground, so she never even saw it.

As she and some of the boy's family prayed over the child, an unknown man walked up and said he was a doctor. He soon said not to worry because he was getting a pulse. Later the boy was life-flighted to a hospital and amazingly released within three days. His doctor said the boy had tire tracks on his chest! It was truly a miracle that he survived.

Not only did God protect the child, but He also

protected Marie. The boy's family decided to sue her even though she wasn't at fault. Almost a year later, they agreed to settle for their hospital bills only. Marie was vindicated. God had definitely shown Marie His protection firsthand, and He will do the same for you.

(Based on a true story)

Record an instance where God protected you or your family. Thank Him for it.

_____

_____

_____

_____

_____

_____

_____

_____

_____

_____

_____

_____

Rest

Father in Heaven,

I am so tired and weary. Life has become a treadmill of endless activity with no end in sight. No matter how much I do, there is always more to be done, and now I am exhausted.

At some point I have to stop and rest, or I am going to burn out. As my Good Shepherd, give me wisdom to know when and how to do this. Restore my soul as I bask in Your presence beside the still waters. Refresh, revive, and restore me that I may serve You with gladness.

In Jesus' name,
Amen.

"Six days a week are for your daily duties and
your regular work, but the seventh day is a day of Sabbath
rest before the Lord your God. On that day you are to do
no work of any kind. . . . For in six days the Lord made the
heaven, earth, and sea, and everything in them,
and rested the seventh day; so he blessed the Sabbath day
and set it aside for rest."

EXODUS 20:9–11 TLB

He said, "My Presence will go with you,
and I will give you rest."

EXODUS 33:14 NKJV

My people will abide in a peaceful habitation,
in secure dwellings, and in quiet resting places.

ISAIAH 32:18 NRSV

"Ask for the old paths, where the good way is,
And walk in it;
Then you will find rest for your souls."

JEREMIAH 6:16 NKJV

My soul finds rest in God alone.

PSALM 62:1 NIV

Rest awhile and run a mile.

PALSGRAVE

HAVE YOU EVER EXPERIENCED THE "TYRANNY OF THE CLOCK"?

The minute hand seems to move faster as your deadlines swiftly approach. Your unaccomplished tasks still continue to pile up—phone calls to return, bills to be paid, laundry to be done, and dinner to be prepared.

The tyranny of the clock can easily steal the enjoyment out of our lives. Daily hassles eat up our time and energy and leave us feeling drained and exhausted: "Hurry up, or we'll be late." "I've only got five minutes to get across town to my appointment!" "You want this project done by when?" These kinds of pressures are normal, but when they begin to build up and take over your life, it's time to slow down and get some rest.

Research has shown that the human body needs from six to nine hours of restful sleep each night in order to function properly. When this amount is shortened, the body is robbed of hormones we need to live healthy lives.

Jesus knew how important rest is. He spoke words that are just as real for us today as they were for His disciples two thousand years ago: "Come with me by yourselves to a quiet place and get some rest" (Mark 6:31 NIV). He knew that people weren't meant to handle the stresses of life without taking a breather now and then.

The Bible says, "God gives rest to his loved ones" (Psalm 127:2 NLT). He longs for you to come to Him and receive the strength and the rest you need to carry on.

When was the last time you got a good night's sleep?

_____

_____

_____

_____

_____

_____

_____

_____

_____

_____

_____

_____

_____

_____

_____

Self-control

Heavenly Father,

Self-control is one of those disciplines I'd rather not think about, but I know it's important and I need to develop it in my life. Will You help me?

When I am tempted to fly off the handle or eat too much, remind me to use self-control. Help me to become more aware of Your presence in me so that I can draw from Your strength. Help me to remember that self-control is not meant to put me into bondage, but it will produce a productive and fulfilling life when I yield to it.

In Jesus' name,
Amen.

We should not be like other people. We should not be
sleeping, but we should be awake and have self-control.

1 Thessalonians 5:6 ICB

Be self-controlled and alert. Your enemy the devil prowls
around like a roaring lion looking for someone to devour.
Resist him, standing firm in the faith.

1 Peter 5:8–9 NIV

Let us be self-controlled, putting on faith and love as a
breastplate, and the hope of salvation as a helmet.

1 Thessalonians 5:8 NIV

The grace of God that brings salvation has appeared
to all men. It teaches us to say "No" to ungodliness and
worldly passions, and to live self-controlled, upright
and godly lives in this present age.

Titus 2:11–12 NIV

Learn the truth and never reject it.
Get wisdom, self-control and understanding.

Proverbs 23:23 ICB

*No man is such a conqueror
as the man who has defeated himself.*

Henry Ward Beecher

INIGO DE LOYOLA, the founder of the Jesuits, was a man who took spiritual discipline seriously. A former soldier who prided himself on his military discipline, Loyola realized that his personal life (which often consisted of gambling, brawling, and sword fighting) was in need of a serious change. While recuperating from an injury, he was given a copy of the Bible and came to know the grace of God and the love of Christ. However, the old desires of his heart and his unhealthy habits soon returned. What was he to do?

The more he grew in his faith, the more Loyola realized the value of self-control. He eventually decided to incorporate the discipline he had learned as a soldier into his spiritual life. Through this discipline and self-control, he finally discovered the peace and satisfaction in life he desired.

The more mature you grow in your faith, the more you will understand the blessings of self-control: When you decline that extra piece of cheesecake or decide not to splurge on those new shoes, the benefits are obvious. But when you begin to practice spiritual self-control, the blessings of God will begin to be poured out on your life.

The Bible tells us that our self-control comes from God's Spirit living in us: "The Spirit that God has given us does not make us timid; instead, his Spirit fills us with power, love, and self-control" (2 Timothy 1:7 GNT). Ask God today to give you the self-control you need to live a life that is pleasing to Him. He is more than willing to provide it—and bless you richly in the process.

In what areas of your life do you most need to practice self-control?

Children

Dear God,

As a Father, You know what a blessing children are. Jesus lovingly embraced and blessed them. I, too, want to bless children and pour myself into them.

Help me to be sensitive to what individual children need most, and enable me to effectively point them to You. Let my Christian walk serve as a shining example that they may desire to know and serve You throughout their lives. Open their eyes to see the hidden riches of Your Word and reveal Yourself to them so they can have a fruitful, personal relationship with You.

In Jesus' name,
Amen.

I will tell the children about your power;
I will tell those who live after me about your might.

PSALM 71:18 NCV

[The Lord our God] gives children to the woman who has
none. He makes her a happy mother.

PSALM 113:9 ICB

Don't you see that children are GOD's best gift?
the fruit of the womb his generous legacy?
Like a warrior's fistful of arrows
are the children of a vigorous youth.

PSALM 127:3–4 MSG

Your children will be like young olive trees
around your table. This is how the LORD will
bless the person who fears him.

PSALM 128:3–4 GWT

[Jesus said,] "Let the children come to me,
and do not stop them, because the Kingdom of God
belongs to such as these." Then he took the children in his
arms . . . and blessed them.

MARK 10:14, 16 GNT

A mother's pride, a father's joy.
SIR WALTER SCOTT

 CHILDREN ARE ONE OF LIFE'S GREATEST BLESSINGS. They can bring a spark of sunshine to the most dismal day with their cheerful spirits and unquenchable energy.

If you already have children, remember to express your thanks to God for blessing you with them. Even in the midst of life's hustle and bustle, take time to appreciate the joy they bring to your day.

Or perhaps you're still waiting to enjoy the blessing of children. Even if you don't have children of your own, there are many ways you can enjoy the pleasures of being a part of a child's life. Maybe you have a friend or sibling who has children and would be more than happy to loan them to you for a special afternoon out. Not only will you be blessed, but you'll be a blessing to the children by letting them know that they are important to you. You'll form special memories with them and provide their parents with a welcome break.

Some other good ways to get involved in the lives of children are to volunteer in the children's department at your church or to become a Big Sister to a child in need of a positive adult role model and friend. Whether you're longing for children or unsure as to whether that road is for you, participating in such activities will help you grow and get to know yourself.

And it will enable you to be a great blessing to others along the way.

In what way, if any, is God leading you to become involved in the life of a child?

Commitment

Heavenly Father,

I want to be a person of my word like You are. Your Word is good all the time, no matter what. Because of that, I can trust You with my whole heart.

Before I make commitments, help me to see situations clearly so I don't make promises I won't be able to fulfill. Teach me when to say yes and when to say no and how to be led by Your Spirit rather than by needs alone. Once I do commit, empower me to follow through joyfully so that I may be a blessing.

In Jesus' name,
Amen.

The eyes of the LORD range throughout the earth to
strengthen those whose hearts are fully committed to him.

2 CHRONICLES 16:9 NIV

What happens when we live God's way? . . . We develop
a willingness to stick with things. . . . We find ourselves
involved in loyal commitments.

GALATIANS 5:22 MSG

If you make a promise to God, don't be slow to keep it. . . .
It is better not to promise anything than to
promise something and not do it.

ECCLESIASTES 5:4–5 NCV

LORD, who may enter your Temple?
Who may worship on Zion, your sacred hill?
Those who obey God in everything
and always do what is right,
whose words are true and sincere. . . .
They always do what they promise,
no matter how much it may cost.

PSALM 15:1–2, 4 GNT

He who lightly assents will seldom keep his word.

CHINESE PROVERB

REMEMBER THE OLD SAYING from Don Quixote: "An honest man's word is as good as his bond"? People in former years actually shook hands to seal a deal instead of having their attorneys draw up intricate papers to sign. People got married for life, and when bad times came, they just stuck it out. When people made a commitment, they kept it.

This character quality (commitment) seems to have gone out of style with poodle skirts and saddle oxford shoes! Today a lot of people enter marriage with the notion that if they're not happy, they'll just get a divorce. They sign leases and then break them. They buy cars and don't pay for them. Our society doesn't seem to know what this word *commitment* means anymore.

That's why God needs us as Christians to be an example of His trustworthiness. When we make a commitment and keep it, we are showing others what God is like. When God makes a commitment, you can bank on it! God doesn't just bail out when things get tough! And we shouldn't either.

Keeping your commitments brings three rewards. First of all, it teaches us to count the cost before we make a pledge. If we know that we are going to keep it no matter what, we will think long and hard before we say yes to something. Second, we feel good about ourselves and have no guilt. Third, and most important, we please God. The Bible says that a godly man "swears to his own hurt" (Psalm 15:4 NASB). In other words, he keeps his oath even when it costs him. Why not let these rewards motivate you to keep your commitments?

Ask God to help you keep all your commitments. If you have overcommitted yourself, ask Him for mercy and guidance. He will either show you His way out or He will give you the strength to keep your pledge.

_____

_____

_____

_____

_____

_____

_____

_____

_____

_____

_____

Conflict in the Home

Heavenly Father,

Home is supposed to be a refuge from the storms of life, but right now conflict is brewing in ours. It breaks my heart when sharp words are exchanged and strife has its way.

Father, minister to each of our hearts and bring us to a place of forgiveness, cooperation, and unity. Help us to communicate clearly to one another, to avoid misunderstanding, to overlook offenses, and to resolve our differences. As we begin to work together as a team, shower Your blessings upon us so that our family will shine brightly for You.

In Jesus' name,
Amen.

How very good and pleasant it is
when kindred live together in unity! . . .
For there the LORD ordained his blessing,
life forevermore.

PSALM 133:1, 3 NRSV

Don't be quick to fly off the handle.
Anger boomerangs. You can spot a fool by the lumps on
his head.

ECCLESIASTES 7:9 MSG

Hate starts quarrels,
but love covers every wrong.

PROVERBS 10:12 GWT

A gentle answer will calm a person's anger,
but an unkind answer will cause more anger.

PROVERBS 15:1 NCV

Starting a quarrel is like a leak in a dam.
So stop the quarrel before a fight breaks out.

PROVERBS 17:14 ICB

It takes two to keep conflict going.

ON HER GOLDEN WEDDING anniversary, an elderly woman revealed the secret of her long and happy marriage. "On my wedding day, I decided to choose ten of my husband's faults, which, for the sake of our marriage, I would overlook," she explained.

A guest asked her to name some of the faults. "To tell the truth," she replied, "I never did get around to listing them. But whenever my husband did something that made me hopping mad, I would say to myself, *Lucky for him that's one of the ten!*"

Conflicts with our spouses, children, and other family members are unavoidable. As someone once said, "If two people agreed on everything, a boring life that would be." But the way you handle conflicts says a lot about you, your relationship with God, and the fruit of the Spirit that is operating (or not!) in your life.

Galatians 5:22 and 23 tell us of the characteristics that should be evident in the life of a Christian—and in a Christian household: "When the Holy Spirit controls our lives, he will produce this kind of fruit in us: love, joy, peace, patience, kindness, goodness, faithfulness, gentleness, and self-control" (NLT). When you and your family members are controlled by love, patience, kindness, and self-control, not only will your household be filled with peace but your family will be a wonderful example of God's love to everyone around you.

Which fruit of the Spirit is most evident in your family's life?

Dating

Father in Heaven,

I need Your help in the area of dating and relationships with men. Only You know what is in the heart of a man and what is best for me. Lead me away from situations where I would be tempted to fall into sexual sin, and deliver me from men who are not capable of having a mature and healthy Christian relationship.

I want to date in a way that pleases You and that enriches both my life and that of anyone I go out with. I trust You for Your very best.

In Jesus' name,
Amen.

GOD said, "It's not good for the Man to be alone;
I'll make him a helper, a companion."

GENESIS 2:18 MSG

Trust in the LORD with all your heart,
and do not rely on your own insight.
In all your ways acknowledge him,
and he will make straight your paths.

PROVERBS 3:5–6 NRSV

Do not be yoked together with unbelievers. For what do
righteousness and wickedness have in common? Or what
fellowship can light have with darkness? . . . What does a
believer have in common with an unbeliever?

2 CORINTHIANS 6:14–15 NIV

Run from sex sin. No other sin affects the body as this one
does. . . . Your body is the home of the Holy Spirit God
gave you. . . . So use every part of your body to give glory
back to God, because he owns it.

1 CORINTHIANS 6:18–20 TLB

*God always gives His very best to those
who leave the choice with Him.*

JAMES HUDSON TAYLOR

WHEN JAMES GILMORE SAILED FOR CHINA IN 1870, he was young, strong, and in need of a wife. He plunged into reopening the London Missionary Society's work in Mongolia, but with no one to lean on. "Companions I can scarcely hope to meet," he wrote, "and the feeling of being alone comes over me." The pain deepened when his proposal to a Scotch girl was rejected. "I then put myself and the direction of this affair—I mean the finding of a wife—into God's hands, asking Him to look me out one, a good one, too."

Eventually James heard of a young girl, Emily Prankard, a friend of a friend, and somehow he knew that God had answered his prayer. But he still turned the situation over to God: "I have put the whole matter into the hands of God," he wrote, "asking Him, if it be best, to bring her, and if it not be best, to keep her away, and He can manage the whole thing well." James eventually did marry Emily, and they labored faithfully side by side for years, reaching northern China for Christ.

James's attitude is a good one to have when dating. While it is easy to get caught up in the outward appearance of a person, or in how he makes you feel, the real question is, what does God think about your relationship? Like James, when you put the whole matter into His hands and realize that He is more than capable of bringing just the right special someone into your life at just the right time, you will be amazed at how His plans for you will unfold.

What qualities are you looking for in a mate?

_____

_____

_____

_____

_____

_____

_____

_____

_____

_____

_____

_____

_____

_____

❋

Divorce

Heavenly Father,

Never did I dream when I walked down that aisle that someday I would be divorced, yet now I am. Will I ever recover? Heal my broken heart, God, and remove the guilt that overwhelms me.

In the midst of my concerns, I choose to trust You with my future. Do with it—do with me—what You will. Only You can take something as tragic as divorce and turn it around for good, and I ask You to do that today. Thank You for a fresh start and a future that will glorify You.

In Jesus' name,
Amen.

When you draw close to God, God will draw close to you.

JAMES 4:8 TLB

It is good to sing psalms to our God. . . .
He is the healer of the brokenhearted.
He is the one who bandages their wounds.

PSALM 147:1, 3 GWT

Do not remember the former things,
or consider the things of old.
I am about to do a new thing;
now it springs forth, do you not perceive it?
I will make a way in the wilderness
and rivers in the desert.

ISAIAH 43:18–19 NRSV

You meant to hurt me.
But God turned your evil into good.

GENESIS 50:20 ICB

The mercy of our God is very tender,
and heaven's dawn is about to break upon us.

LUKE 1:78 TLB

*Mishaps are like knives that either serve us or cut us as we
grasp them by the blade or by the handle.*

JAMES RUSSELL LOWELL

IF YOU'VE GONE THROUGH A DIVORCE, you know the anguish it brings. You hurt deeply, and you also worry about the effect it will have upon your children.

If you're in the midst of this tragedy right now, God wants to help you. Only He understands exactly how you feel. He longs to heal your broken heart so that you can survive this sad event and go on to build another life. He also wants to protect your kids so that they emerge from this as unscathed as possible.

The thing you must do is this: you must not allow your pain and anger to affect you in such a way that you turn from God instead of toward Him. He really is your hope at this time. He is the only One who can turn what is meant for evil into good.

We all have the tendency to withdraw when facing great loss. We fear the pain may destroy us, so we choose to escape it. We may drink too much, we may want to be alone, or we may take our anger out on those around us—none of these solve the problem.

The only permanent solution is dealing with the pain. When a doctor peels back a scab to clean out infection, it hurts. But when infection is exposed and medicated, it can heal. That holds true with your hurting heart. Be honest with God. Tell Him how you feel. Give Him all your anger—He won't reject you. Ask Him to help you deal with the pain in a manner that pleases Him. He wants to help you. Will you let Him?

Write a letter to God expressing everything you feel. Don't hold anything back. Let Him replace your anger with His peace.

_____

_____

_____

_____

_____

_____

_____

_____

_____

_____

_____

_____

_____

Faith

Father in Heaven,

The fact that I believe in You is evidence that there is faith in my heart, but I want my faith to grow. I want to have faith like the patriarchs of old, who not only believed in You but were unmoved by circumstances and received what You promised.

Direct me in Your Word so that my faith may increase, so that doubt will be overcome, and so that I can win the good fight of faith. Take my faith in You and Your promises and accomplish Your will in my life.

In the name of Jesus,
Amen.

[Jesus said,] "Have faith in God! If you have faith in God and don't doubt, you can tell this mountain to get up and jump into the sea, and it will. Everything you ask for in prayer will be yours, if you only have faith."

MARK 11:22–24 CEV

Faith means being sure of the things we hope for and knowing that something is real even if we do not see it.

HEBREWS 11:1 NCV

[Abraham's] faith did not leave him, and he did not doubt God's promise; his faith filled him with power, and he gave praise to God. He was absolutely sure that God would be able to do what he had promised.

ROMANS 4:20–21 GNT

Fight the good fight of faith.

1 TIMOTHY 6:12 NCV

Remember those who led you,
who spoke the word of God to you; and considering the result of their conduct, imitate their faith.

HEBREWS 13:7 NASB

For what is faith unless it is to believe what you do not see?

SAINT AUGUSTINE

A FAMOUS TIGHTROPE WALKER ONCE went to Niagara Falls and stretched his rope across the thunderous currents from Canada to the United States. Before the breathless multitudes, he walked, then ran, across the falls. He did the same blindfolded, with drums rolling. Then, still blindfolded, he pushed a wheelbarrow across the falls.

The crowds went wild, and the aerialist shouted to them, "Who believes I can push a man in this wheelbarrow across these falls?"

A gentleman in the front waved his hands, shouting, "I do! I believe!"

"Then," said the walker, "come and get in the wheelbarrow."

To no surprise, the man's intellectual assent failed to translate into personal belief.

Many of us will loudly proclaim our belief in God and His promises, but when it comes to actually putting them into action in our lives, we waiver. Jesus once encountered a man like that. His child was sick, and he went to Jesus for help. Jesus assured him that, through faith, his child could be made well: "If you can believe, all things are possible" (Mark 9:23 NKJV).

The man's famous answer echoes many of our own

prayers today: "Lord, I believe; help my unbelief!" (v. 24 NKJV).

Do you need more faith today? Do you need to put action to the faith you already have? Ask the Lord to increase your faith and to help you find ways to live it out—and then expect your faith to bring great things to pass in your life.

In what areas of your life do you need to pray the prayer: "Lord, I believe; help my unbelief"?

_____

_____

_____

_____

_____

_____

_____

_____

_____

_____

_____

Finances

Heavenly Father,

Help me to have a right mindset toward finances. I don't want the "love of money" to control or guide me, yet I need money to function in this world. Help me to be a good steward of the finances You bring into my hands. Show me how much and where to give, how much to save, and how to manage what is left.

If ever my heart becomes greedy or selfish, bring it to my attention so that I may correct my attitude. I want to honor You in all my financial dealings.

In Jesus' name,
Amen.

[Jesus said,] "The thing you should want most is God's kingdom and doing what God wants. Then all these other things you need will be given to you."

MATTHEW 6:33 NCV

The blessing of the LORD makes one rich,
And He adds no sorrow with it.

PROVERBS 10:22 NKJV

God will make you rich in every way so that you can always give freely. And your giving through us will cause many to give thanks to God. This service that you do helps the needs of God's people. It is also bringing more and more thanks to God.

2 CORINTHIANS 9:11–12 ICB

"Give, and it will be given to you. A good measure, pressed down, shaken together and running over, will be poured into your lap. For with the measure you use, it will be measured to you."

LUKE 6:38 NIV

"Where your treasure is, there your heart will be also."

MATTHEW 6:21 NRSV

Having money is fine as long as money doesn't have you.

THE WAY WE HANDLE OUR MONEY IS PERHAPS THE TRUEST INDICATOR OF THE SPIRITUAL CONDITION OF OUR HEARTS. Maybe that is why the Scriptures place such an emphasis on finances. The Bible contains more than five hundred references to prayer and almost five hundred references to faith, but did you know that there are more than two thousand references to money and possessions?

Out of thirty-eight parables that Jesus told in the Gospels, sixteen deal with how we handle our money. Jesus said more about money and possessions than about heaven and hell combined. One out of every ten verses in the Gospels deals with money or possessions—288 in the entire four Gospels.

It sounds as if the way we handle our finances is a priority to God, doesn't it? That's because what we do with money gives a clear picture of our relationship with God. If we are good stewards of what God has given us and freely share with others, it demonstrates a heart in tune with God's purposes and heart; but if we greedily hoard what we have, or spend it wildly or frivolously, it reveals a heart of selfishness.

While money is important, it can't give us the things we really need. It will buy a bed, but not sleep; books, but not brains; clothes, but not beauty; a house, but not a home; medicine, but not health; amusements, but not happiness. On the other hand, when we keep our focus on God's priorities and handle the money He gives us with wisdom and generosity, we will be blessed beyond measure.

How can you be more generous with the money God has given you?

Friendship

Dear Father,

Friendship is truly a gift from You. Thank You for the friends You have already given me as well as the ones You will bring into my life in the future. May You be the center of all of these relationships. May we encourage one another to seek You and grow in You. May our words and actions honor You.

Use me to be a friend to the friendless, to speak encouraging words and point them to You. You are the best friend any of us could ever have, and I love You for it.

In Jesus' name,
Amen.

Two are better than one,
because they have a good return for their work:
If one falls down,
his friend can help him up.
But pity the man who falls
and has no one to help him up!

ECCLESIASTES 4:9–10 NIV

The righteous person is a guide to his friend,
but the path of the wicked leads them astray.

PROVERBS 12:26 GNT

A friend loves you all the time.

PROVERBS 17:17 ICB

You use steel to sharpen steel,
and one friend sharpens another.

PROVERBS 27:17 MSG

[Jesus said,] "No one has greater love than this,
to lay down one's life for one's friends."

JOHN 15:13 NRSV

The worst solitude is to have no true friendships.

FRANCIS BACON

FRIENDSHIP IS ONE OF THE SWEETEST BLESSINGS we can experience in life. Samuel Taylor Coleridge once wrote a poem titled "Youth and Age" with the line, "Friendship is a sheltering tree." What a wonderful word picture! Friends are those whose lives are like branches. They provide shade, and they provide refuge from the demanding, irritating, and searing rays of the hot sun. You can find comfort when you are with them. You can find strength by being near them. They are treelike because they bear fruit that provides nourishment and encouragement.

The Bible also tells us of the blessing of friendship: "The heartfelt counsel of a friend is as sweet as perfume and incense" (Proverbs 27:9 NLT); "There are 'friends' who pretend to be friends, but there is a friend who sticks closer than a brother" (Proverbs 18:24 TLB).

There is nothing quite like the feeling of knowing that you have a close friend who will always be by your side—someone with whom you can share the intimate details of your life and know that she will listen and understand; someone upon whom you can depend to give you good advice and support you in the love and grace of God.

Take some time today to thank God for the friends He has placed in your life. And, if you are in need of a friend, ask Him to provide the relationships you need to help you grow in your walk with God and become who He wants you to be.

How can you be a friend to someone this week?

Gossip

Heavenly Father,

It is so tempting to gossip. There are times when "news" is right on the tip of my tongue, begging to be released. But I know that gossip—even in the form of "concern"—disappoints You. Surely it breaks Your heart when I betray another in that way.

Father, forgive me for the times I've let juicy tidbits escape my lips, and help me to restrain myself in the future. I want to be a trustworthy friend whom others can turn to in times of need, a godly woman who will be faithful to pray.

In Jesus' name,
Amen.

Keep your mouth closed and you'll stay out of trouble.

PROVERBS 21:23 TLB

A gadabout gossip can't be trusted with a secret,
but someone of integrity won't violate a confidence.

PROVERBS 11:13 MSG

The Lord . . . is the friend of all
who can be trusted.
Be sensible and don't tell
everything you know—
only fools spread
foolishness everywhere.

PROVERBS 12:22–23 CEV

When you run out of wood, the fire goes out;
when the gossip ends, the quarrel dies down.

PROVERBS 26:20 MSG

Though some tongues just love the taste of gossip,
Christians have better uses for language than that.

EPHESIANS 5:4 MSG

*A cruel story runs on wheels,
and every hand oils the wheels as they run.*

OUIDA

MILDRED FISTER'S BEAUTY PARLOR IN JEFFERSON, IOWA, HAS AN UNUSUAL RULE. Mildred refuses to allow gossip. A columnist for the *Des Moines Register* reacted this way: "This is a beauty parlor, for goodness' sake, one of those places women come to say things—loving, kind, unkind, and, sure, maybe downright nasty—about their friends and neighbors, whether it's true or not. It's as basic in a beauty parlor as a blow-dry. Isn't it?"

But Mildred stands firm. There is absolutely no talking about other people in her shop. Talk about you and yours if you like . . . but in the meantime, no gossip. You would think that Mildred doesn't have to worry about keeping secrets—but she actually knows the entire town's secrets because she's a friend to everybody who comes in the place. They know she can be trusted.

"Sometimes people don't have anybody to talk to," she said. "So they confide in me. They tell me things about themselves. They know I'll never repeat what they say."

That's better than gossip. It's called friendship.

The next time you are tempted to gossip about someone, remember Mildred's philosophy: The best way to make a friend—and to keep a friend—is to show that you can be trusted, no matter what. The evangelist Leonard Ravenhill also had a good insight: "We never pray for folks we gossip about, and we never gossip about the folks for whom we pray!" Next time you're tempted to gossip about someone, say a prayer instead.

The Bible says that to have friends, we must be friendly ourselves. (See Proverbs 18:24 NKJV.) Gossip separates and divides, but true friendship brings people together in love.

Whom are you most tempted to gossip about? How can you pray for them instead?

Humility

Heavenly Father,

Humility is such a vital attribute, and I want to develop it in my life. Not false humility—which is really just pride masquerading as humility—but true, godly humility that makes me look like Jesus.

Without You I am nothing and I cannot do anything of lasting value. But in You and because of You, Father, I can accomplish what You have called me to do. Help me to recognize pride when it tries to seduce me, and help me to maintain a humble heart, for it is then that You are truly glorified.

In Jesus' name,
Amen.

The LORD . . . is gracious to humble people.

PROVERBS 3:33-34 GWT

The reward for humility and fear of the LORD
is riches and honor and life.

PROVERBS 22:4 NRSV

Pride ends in a fall, while humility brings honor.

PROVERBS 29:23 TLB

Are there any of you who are wise and understanding?
You are to prove it by your good life, by your good deeds
performed with humility and wisdom.

JAMES 3:13 GNT

You save humble people,
but you bring down a conceited look.

PSALM 18:27 GWT

I [the LORD] will renew the spirit of those who are humble.

ISAIAH 57:15 GWT

There is no humiliation for humility.

JOSEPH ROUX

MISSIONARY HUDSON TAYLOR was one of the greatest missionaries that China had ever seen. Founder of the China Inland Mission, he spent five years translating the New Testament into the Ningpo dialect. He established 205 mission stations in China and saw over 125,000 Chinese people come to Christ in his lifetime.

During one of his trips to Melbourne, Australia, Hudson Taylor was scheduled to speak at a large Presbyterian church about his work. The moderator of the service introduced the missionary in eloquent and glowing terms. He told the large congregation all that Taylor had accomplished in China and then presented him as "our illustrious guest."

Taylor stood quietly for a moment, and then he opened his message by saying, "Dear friends, I am the little servant of an illustrious Master."

It is sometimes easy to be tempted to brag about our talents, our skills, or even the ministries that God has blessed us with. But we must always keep in mind who is the Giver of these gifts and give Him the praise for what He is able to do through us. Hudson Taylor went on to say in his message: "I think God was looking for a little man, little enough so that He could show Himself strong through him. A man can receive nothing except it be given him from heaven." John the Baptist had the same idea when he said of Jesus: "He must increase, but I must decrease" (John 3:30 NKJV).

Are you "little enough" to be used by God? Or is your pride getting in the way? Ask God for the humility you need to be a vessel easily available for the Master's use.

How can you make God greater in your life?

_____

_____

_____

_____

_____

_____

_____

_____

_____

_____

_____

_____

_____

Hurts and Offenses

Father God,

I've gotten my feelings hurt. You saw what happened. Shouldn't I be offended?

I know the answer to that question, and I ask You to forgive me for trying to nurse a grudge. I turn this hurt over to You and ask You to heal the wound.

So that I won't become bitter or give any place to the evil one, I yield to Your forgiveness and love. I choose to let my offender off the hook. In fact, I go a step further and ask You to bless the person who has wronged me.

In Jesus' name,
Amen.

Never get revenge. Never hold a grudge
against any of your people. Instead, love your neighbor
as you love yourself. I am the LORD.

LEVITICUS 19:18 GWT

[Love] is not irritable or touchy. It does not hold grudges
and will hardly even notice when others do it wrong.

1 CORINTHIANS 13:5 TLB

Be even-tempered, content with second place,
quick to forgive an offense. Forgive as quickly and
completely as the Master forgave you.

COLOSSIANS 3:13 MSG

Watch out that no bitterness takes root among you,
for as it springs up it causes deep trouble, hurting many in
their spiritual lives.

HEBREWS 12:15 TLB

[Jesus said,] "Love your enemies. Let them bring out the
best in you, not the worst. When someone gives you a hard
time, respond with the energies of prayer."

MATTHEW 5:44 MSG

When you hold a grudge, it ends up holding you.

EVERY DAY YOU GET OPPORTUNI-TIES TO GET OFFENDED. Someone breaks in front of you at the grocery checkout. Someone cuts you off in traffic. Easy.

But what about your reaction when a loved one snaps at you or a friend gossips about you? Harder to handle. It's easier to be offended and then to want to hold on to that offense. Even an initial reaction of anger and hurt is justified, along with being upset. But we do not have the right to let those feelings dominate our lives.

When asked by a disciple how many times he should forgive, Jesus' answer was "seventy times seven" (Matthew 18:22 KJV). Obviously Jesus knew just how often we would need to forgive and, on the other hand, how often we need to be forgiven. Jesus never said to deny how you feel—He just said to forgive.

Here are a few tips for you the next time you feel hurt by another:

- Give your hurt to the Lord. Pray for wisdom in handling the situation.

- If the Lord directs you to talk to the person, speak to them privately and in love, without anger.

- Use this template for your discussion. "When you said

this, I felt hurt. I was embarrassed, humiliated," or whatever your true feeling was.

- Do not accuse them. It will only put them on the defensive.

No matter what the result, ask the Lord to help you forgive them. Forgiveness is not saying the action was right. It is your releasing them from your judgment and placing them in God's hands—because He is the only true judge. And wouldn't you want them to do the same for you?

Are you holding on to an offense against someone? What do you need to do to resolve it?

_____

_____

_____

_____

_____

_____

_____

_____

_____

_____

Integrity

Heavenly Father,

One of Your greatest attributes is that You are true to Your Word. You never lie or color the truth. Because of it, we can always count on You.

Oh, how I want that to be said of me—especially by You. I want to be someone You can count on to be a person of integrity, one who is consistently true to my word.

Sometimes it is easier to tell "little white lies" instead of being honest. Help me to resist that temptation so I can be a person of integrity who pleases You.

In the name of Your Son,
Amen.

Vindicate me, O LORD, according to my
righteousness and my integrity that is in me.
O let the evil of the wicked come to an end,
but establish the righteous;
For the righteous God tries the hearts and minds.
My shield is with God,
Who saves the upright in heart.

PSALM 7:8–10 NASB

I know, my God, that you test the heart
and are pleased with integrity.

1 CHRONICLES 29:17 NIV

You have upheld me because of my integrity,
and set me in your presence forever.

PSALM 41:12 NRSV

Whoever walks in integrity walks securely.

PROVERBS 10:9 NRSV

The integrity of the upright guides them.

PROVERBS 11:3 NRSV

Character is much easier kept than recovered.

THOMAS PAINE

ALLEN C. EMERY WAS A SUCCESSFUL BUSINESSMAN who also served as an officer for many evangelical organizations, including the Billy Graham Evangelistic Association as the board chairman. For years he and his wife hosted a Bible club at their Massachusetts church that drew up to one hundred young people each week.

Emery was greatly influenced by the integrity and honesty of his father. Once his dad lost a pair of fine German binoculars. He collected the insurance money, only to find the binoculars a year later. Immediately he sent a check to the company and eventually received a letter back stating that this seldom occurred and that they were encouraged by his honesty. Although it was a small thing, Emery's father set an example that influenced his children throughout their lifetimes.

Integrity is not a word we hear much about these days. But although it is not the norm for most, it should always be the rule of the day for Christians. We should seek to be like Hanani, a builder of the ancient walls of Jerusalem, about whom the Bible says: "He was a man of integrity and feared God more than most men do" (Nehemiah 7:2 NIV). Ask God to show you those areas of your life in which the walls of integrity need shoring up. He's promised to help you walk with integrity in this

154

world—and as the God of integrity Himself, He always keeps His Word.

What does the word integrity mean to you?

_____

_____

_____

_____

_____

_____

_____

_____

_____

_____

_____

_____

_____

_____

_____

_____

_____

Jealousy

Father in Heaven,

Jealousy is such an ugly emotion, and I do not like it in me. I want to be happy for those who are blessed, not secretly seething inside.

Help me to keep my eyes on You and to remember that You are no respecter of persons. You want to bless all of Your children—including me. Forgive me for not keeping this in mind and for allowing jealousy to build a wall between me and others. I choose to rejoice with those who rejoice, knowing that You have good things in store for me too.

In the name of Your Son,
Amen.

Love never is envious nor boils over with jealousy.

1 Corinthians 13:4 AMP

If you are bitterly jealous and filled with self-centered ambition, don't brag. Don't say that you are wise when it isn't true. That kind of wisdom doesn't come from above. It belongs to this world. It is self-centered and demonic. Wherever there is jealousy and rivalry, there is disorder and every kind of evil.

James 3:14–16 GWT

When you are jealous and quarrel among yourselves, aren't you influenced by your corrupt nature and living by human standards?

1 Corinthians 3:3 GWT

Be happy with those who are happy.

Romans 12:15 GNT

Let us live in a right way, like people who belong to the day. . . . There should be . . . no fighting or jealousy. But clothe yourselves with the Lord Jesus Christ and forget about satisfying your sinful self.

Romans 13:13–14 NCV

Jealousy will be the ruin of you.

Martial

THE FAMOUS BIBLE TEACHER F. B. MEYER OFTEN MINISTERED AT DWIGHT L. MOODY'S BIBLE CONFERENCES in Northfield, Massachusetts, and he always drew great crowds. But when the equally famous G. Campbell Morgan began preaching at Northfield as well, his stirring Bible studies attracted larger audiences. Meyer confessed to some of his closest friends that he was tempted to feel envious of Morgan. But he had a remedy in mind: "The only way I can conquer my feelings," he said, "is to pray for him daily, which I do."

The Bible has a lot to say about the emotion of jealousy: "Surely resentment destroys the fool, and jealousy kills the simple" (Job 5:2 NLT). The writer of Proverbs gave this graphic description: "Peace of mind makes the body healthy, but jealousy is like a cancer" (Proverbs 14:30 GNT). And the apostle Peter instructs us: "Rid yourselves, then, of all evil; no more lying or hypocrisy or jealousy or insulting language" (1 Peter 2:1 GNT).

God knew how destructive jealousy can be—that's why He warned against it. But F. B. Meyer had the right solution to his jealousy problem: The more you pray for others, the less likely you are to feel envious of their success, wealth, or possessions. As someone once said: "If I think about your success, plan for your success, pray for your success, genuinely hope for your success, and work for your success, then I will rejoice in your success."

Are you jealous of somebody today? Ask God to pour out His blessing on that person. As you do, your attitude will begin to change, and God's peace, rather than jealousy and envy, will begin to rule in your heart.

In what ways can you express happiness about the success of others?

_____

_____

_____

_____

_____

_____

_____

_____

_____

_____

_____

_____

_____

Judging Others

Heavenly Father,

It is so easy to judge others while at the same time being unaware of my own shortcomings. Forgive me for falling prey to this trap. What others do is between You and them. Remind me to pray for those who err, rather than passing judgment on them. Help me to see people's positive qualities instead of their negative traits.

On the other hand, help me to judge myself so I won't be judged. Point out areas where I need to grow and change so I can keep my heart pure before You.

In Jesus' name,
Amen.

[Jesus said,] "Do not judge, and you will not be judged; and do not condemn, and you will not be condemned; pardon, and you will be pardoned."

LUKE 6:37 NASB

Don't grumble about each other. . . . Are you yourselves above criticism? For see! The great Judge is coming. He is almost here. [Let him do whatever criticizing must be done.]

JAMES 5:9 TLB

[Jesus said,] "Do not judge by appearances."

JOHN 7:24 NRSV

You have no excuse, whoever you are, when you judge others; for in passing judgment on another you condemn yourself, because you, the judge, are doing the very same things.

ROMANS 2:1 NRSV

There is one lawgiver and judge who is able to save and to destroy. So who, then, are you to judge your neighbor?

JAMES 4:12 NRSV

The more one judges, the less one loves.

HONORÉ DE BALZAC

A WOMAN LEFT HER APARTMENT ONE MORNING FOR A TRIP DOWNTOWN. She put on her most fashionable outfit and her favorite perfume and went to catch a bus. As she hurried out the back door, she picked up a small sack of garbage in the kitchen to toss it into the container at the curb on her way to catch the bus. But she was so preoccupied that she forgot about holding the sack of garbage. So, she carried it, along with her other packages, onto the bus.

As she took her seat, she noticed a terrible stench. She opened the window, to no avail. Later, as she shopped, she noticed that the terrible stench was in every store she visited. She couldn't escape the smell and eventually concluded, "The whole world stinks!" Only after she returned home and opened her packages did she realize where the odor was coming from.

Before you begin to point the finger at other people, it is always smart to check out your own packages first. The "stink" you smell may not be from others—it may be your own! Jesus had this to say about judging other people: "Don't pick on people, jump on their failures, criticize their faults—unless, of course, you want the same treatment. That critical spirit has a way of boomeranging" (Matthew 7:1–2 MSG). Jesus was right—make sure you've

162

taken out your own garbage first before you begin to criticize the garbage of the people around you.

Of whom do you tend to be most critical?

_____

_____

_____

_____

_____

_____

_____

_____

_____

_____

_____

_____

_____

_____

_____

Letting Go of the Past

Dear God,

I'm having trouble letting go of the past. Like a vacuum, tormenting thoughts try to suck me back into their grip to prevent me from moving on. I need Your help.

Thank You for the blood of Jesus, which cleanses me from the stain of the past. Lead me to promises in Your Word on which I can focus to keep me moving forward in Your plan. I trust that You are guiding me to brighter days filled with good things. By Your grace, I set my gaze on Jesus and press on.

In the name of Your Son,
Amen.

The Lord says, "Forget what happened before.
Do not think about the past.
Look at the new thing I am going to do.
It is already happening. Don't you see it?"

ISAIAH 43:18–19 ICB

"All the earlier troubles, chaos, and pain
are things of the past, to be forgotten.
Look ahead with joy.
Anticipate what I'm creating."

ISAIAH 65:17–18 MSG

Your new day is dawning.
The glory of the LORD
shines brightly on you.

ISAIAH 60:1 CEV

GOD made my life complete
when I placed all the pieces before him.
When I cleaned up my act,
he gave me a fresh start.

2 SAMUEL 22:21 MSG

*Shut out all of your past except that which will help you
weather your tomorrows.*

SIR WILLIAM OSLER

WHEN THE APOSTLE PAUL spoke of fulfilling God's call upon his life, he admitted that he sometimes failed in that pursuit. But he made a commitment to do one thing. What was that one thing? He said that he would forget the things in the past and focus on what lay ahead. (See Philippians 3:7–14.)

What a valuable lesson for us today. Many of us spend lots of time living in the past, regretting things we've done. We replay scenes over and over again in our minds as if that will somehow erase them. Others of us replay happy scenes from our past so that we do not have to face the present, which may be more painful. Either way, it is a waste of time and energy because we can never go back.

A preacher once said that God designed us to live in twenty-four-hour packets of time. Every day is supposed to be a fresh start. That's encouraging because each day we get to try again. And if we are having struggles, we have the hope that tomorrow may be better. But to enjoy this hope of a new day, you have to say good-bye to yesterday and embrace today.

Doing that may seem impossible to you. You may feel you have blown it so badly that it cannot be fixed. But that's not true. Ask the Lord for His help, for He is merciful and will give you wisdom for your situation. And if you miss the happiness of the past, ask the Lord to help you embrace the joy He longs to give you today. Go ahead, you can trust Him!

What do you need to let go of from the past? Will you do it today?

_____

_____

_____

_____

_____

_____

_____

_____

_____

_____

_____

_____

_____

_____

_____

Marriage

Dear God,

I believe You want us to have a marriage that is heaven on earth. It's easy to get caught up in day-to-day life and let the spark die out, but we didn't get married to just become roommates!

Help us to be mindful of the things that drew us together in the first place and to resolve conflicts that would try to divide us. Show me ways that I can encourage my husband, to help him become all You've destined him to become. Thank You for the gift You've given us in each other.

In Jesus' name,
Amen.

May you rejoice in the wife of your youth.
A loving doe, a graceful deer—
may her breasts satisfy you always,
may you ever be captivated by her love.

PROVERBS 5:18–19 NIV

Let each man of you [without exception] love his wife as
[being in a sense] his very own self; and let the wife see that
she respects and reverences her husband [that she notices
him, regards him, honors him, prefers him, venerates,
and esteems him; and that she defers to him, praises him,
and loves and admires him exceedingly].

EPHESIANS 5:33 AMP

Be kind to each other, tenderhearted,
forgiving one another, just as God has forgiven you
because you belong to Christ.

EPHESIANS 4:32 TLB

This is what I have asked of God for you: that you will be
encouraged and knit together by strong ties of love, and
that you will have the rich experience of knowing Christ.

COLOSSIANS 2:2 TLB

Marriage God's way is heaven on earth.

❀

SALLY REMEMBERED WHEN she and her husband, Steve, were dating. Her heart fluttered every time she was with him—and that was often because he couldn't stay away! One day he brought her flowers—the next day, her favorite candy. Yes, they were in love, and everyone knew it.

Then came the wedding, and they settled into their new life together. Next came jobs, a mortgage, and a couple of kids. The luster of their romance slowly wore away. It was replaced by mundane activities like work, soccer practice, homework, and cleaning house. No wonder they didn't look at each other longingly anymore.

Does this description of their lives sound a little too much like your own? It's easy for the everyday grind to slowly steal the joy and life out of your marriage. You begin to blame one another for what is missing. He doesn't open my door anymore. He never helps out around the house. What you fail to realize is that you are probably not doing the things you used to do either.

When you're dating, your focus is on pleasing one another. If you're not careful, this can change after marriage. Other things can take precedence to the point that you just live under the same roof, putting out the fires of life and not even relating to one another.

So what do you do? Simple. You begin to do the things

you used to do. You write him love letters. You tell him you appreciate him. You do the "little things" that have big results. You show your spouse that you care and your marriage is a priority. It sounds simple, but it worked in the beginning, didn't it?

What are some things you can do to make your mate feel special and loved?

_____

_____

_____

_____

_____

_____

_____

_____

_____

_____

_____

Praise

Heavenly Father,

The last thing I feel like doing right now is praising You—not because I don't love You or think You are worthy to be praised but because negative emotions are weighing me down.

Nevertheless, I am not going to allow these feelings to control me. I choose to praise You in the midst of my difficulties because I trust that You are working on my behalf even now. You are good, loving, faithful, trustworthy, and mighty to deliver me; therefore, I magnify, glorify, exalt, and praise You with my whole heart.

In Jesus' name,
Amen.

Give thanks to the LORD, call on his name;
make known among the nations what he has done.
Sing to him, sing praise to him;
tell of all his wonderful acts.

1 CHRONICLES 16:8–9 NIV

[The Lord] is the one you should praise; he is your God,
who has done great and wonderful things for you, which
you have seen with your own eyes.

DEUTERONOMY 10:21 NCV

"Worship the LORD your God; it is he who will deliver you
from the hand of all your enemies."

2 KINGS 17:39 NIV

I will praise thee, O LORD, with my whole heart; I will
shew forth all thy marvellous works.
I will be glad and rejoice in thee: I will sing praise to thy
name, O thou most High.

PSALM 9:1–2 KJV

The LORD is my strength and my shield; my heart trusted
in him, and I am helped: therefore my heart greatly
rejoiceth; and with my song will I praise him.

PSALM 28:7 KJV

Praise in the midst of trials is an expression of great faith.

WE LIVE IN A WORLD THAT does not always make sense. But when life gets tough, we can always stop and praise God in the midst of it all. To praise God can, at times, seem like the most ineffective action we can take, especially when we are surrounded by challenges and situations beyond our control. So, why should we? The Bible gives us the answer in Hebrews 13:15: "Let us offer the sacrifice of praise to God continually, that is, the fruit of our lips giving thanks to his name" (KJV).

Although praise may be a sacrifice at first, to praise and worship God in the midst of your stormiest days demonstrates your confidence that He is still in control. Such praise, which swells out of your heart and through your lips, professes that you will not let go of your faith no matter what life throws your way.

Martin Luther once said, "The most acceptable service we can do and show unto God and which alone He desires of us is that He be praised of us." While praising God during times of misunderstanding, trials, and hardship may seem foolish to some, it is most often the way out of tribulation.

Will you give God your praise today? Will you tell God that you know who He is, how great and exalted He is, how He is Lord of every aspect of your life? If so, the sacrifice of praise can change your life. It might not change your outward situation immediately, but it will change your attitude. And the declaration of your trust in your God will strengthen your resolve to see things through.

Take a few minutes to praise God for the amazing things He has done in your life.

_____

_____

_____

_____

_____

_____

_____

_____

_____

_____

_____

_____

_____

_____

Purpose

Father in Heaven,

I don't want to walk aimlessly through this life only to discover in eternity that I missed the very purpose for which I was created. Help me to discover and develop the unique gifts You've built into my DNA. Show me where to invest them to bless others.

You said in Your Word that if I would acknowledge You in all my ways, You would direct my paths and make them sure, so I submit to You today. When this life is over, I want to hear You say, "Well done, good and faithful servant."

In Jesus' name,
Amen.

"I know the plans I have for you," declares the LORD,
"plans to prosper you and not to harm you,
plans to give you hope and a future."

JEREMIAH 29:11 NIV

The LORD will fulfill his purpose for me;
your love, O LORD, endures forever.

PSALM 138:8 NIV

Each one has his own gift from God,
one in this manner and another in that.

1 CORINTHIANS 7:7 NKJV

In him we were also chosen, having been predestined
according to the plan of him who works out everything in
conformity with the purpose of his will.

EPHESIANS 1:11 NIV

We are His workmanship, created in Christ Jesus
for good works, which God prepared beforehand
that we should walk in them.

EPHESIANS 2:10 NKJV

Purpose is the rudder that guides the ship.

PURPOSE IS A BUZZWORD THESE DAYS. Everyone wants to know why they're here and what they were put here to do. That's good because it's important. Why? Because we are all going to leave this world one day, and our lives won't end then. In actuality, that will just be the beginning because we are going to live forever. Hard to fathom? It is, and that is why we sometimes don't take it seriously. We become consumed with this life and all its activities and don't consider the fact that the way we live now affects the way we will live in eternity.

So we should live our lives with purpose. What we do here does matter, and our present life will affect eternity. In fact, one of the choices you will make will affect where you spend eternity. If you accept Jesus' provision for your sins in this life, then you will reside with Him forever in the next life. And making this decision fulfills your greatest purpose—to know God. That is why God created us; He wanted a relationship with us.

And after we come to know Him, then our greatest purpose should be to please Him. He has a specific plan for each of us, and as we follow that plan, we will reach others, we will give to God's work, and we will be well-pleasing to Him. We will actually be laying up for ourselves treasures in the next life (Matthew 6:20) because God will reward actions done in obedience to Him (Revelation 22:12).

So, remember that what you do today will affect tomorrow. What kind of eternity are you preparing for?

If you really believed that today will affect your eternity, what would you do differently today?

_____

_____

_____

_____

_____

_____

_____

_____

_____

_____

_____

_____

_____

Reconciliation

Father,

Being separated from You is the worst pain there is, yet that would have been my lot had You not sent Jesus to reconcile me to You. I'm thankful for His blood that bridged the gap so that now we are one.

Even though I will spend eternity with You, I want to make sure that no sin separates me from You for even an hour on earth. When I miss it, help me to be quick to acknowledge my error and to ask for forgiveness. I want to live reconciled to You.

In Jesus' name,
Amen.

God was pleased to have all his fullness dwell in him,
and through him to reconcile to himself all things . . .
by making peace through his blood, shed on the cross.

COLOSSIANS 1:19–20 NIV

We are ambassadors for Christ, since GOD is making
his appeal through us; we entreat you on behalf of Christ,
be reconciled to GOD.

2 CORINTHIANS 5:20 NRSV

If while we were enemies we were reconciled to God
through the death of His Son, much more, having been
reconciled, we shall be saved by His life.

ROMANS 5:10 NASB

If anyone is in Christ, he is a new creation;
the old has gone, the new has come! All this is from God,
who reconciled us to himself through Christ and gave us
the ministry of reconciliation: that God was reconciling the
world to himself in Christ, not counting men's sins against
them. And he has committed to us the
message of reconciliation.

2 CORINTHIANS 5:17–19 NIV

*The door is always open for prodigal sons and daughters to
come home to the Father.*

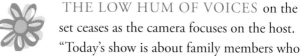 THE LOW HUM OF VOICES on the set ceases as the camera focuses on the host. "Today's show is about family members who have not spoken to each other in years," he says as the audience applauds. Then comes the array of characters who tell their stories, not expecting that backstage sits their family members who have arranged this meeting. As the show progresses, you see all kinds of reactions as the people are reunited—surprise, joy, and anger. But the scene that really warms your heart is the one that shows two sisters who had an argument eight years ago and have not spoken since. They hesitantly walk toward each other, and then their faces soften and they begin to cry. Then they hug each other as they tell each other that they're sorry. There's not a dry eye in the house!

That is a picture of reconciliation. Heart-warming, isn't it?

Well, that is what God did for us. He sent Jesus to break down the barrier between us. Our sin kept us from God, but Jesus' sacrifice paid the debt for our sin. And when we receive the forgiveness Jesus died to give us, we are at peace with God—we are reconciled to Him. Once we become Christians, our relationship with God becomes secure. It is the fellowship that we must maintain.

How do we do that? By simply admitting our sins to

Him when we miss it. This is the place where God wants us to live our lives—a place where there is no need of reconciliation.

Is everything right between you and God? If not, admit it and let Him take you back into the fold.

_____

_____

_____

_____

_____

_____

_____

_____

_____

_____

_____

_____

_____

_____

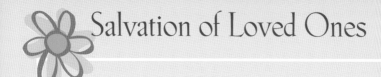

Salvation of Loved Ones

Heavenly Father,

I am so thankful for my salvation, but I also want my loved ones to be saved so we can spend eternity together. Give me wisdom about what to say and what not to say, and help me to lead a life that bears testimony to Your goodness.

Send laborers across the path of each family member to share the Good News, and reveal to my loved ones that Jesus is the Christ, the resurrected Savior. May they all confess Him as Lord so that together we may glorify You throughout eternity.

In the mighty name of Jesus,
Amen.

Try to shine as lights among the people of this world,
as you hold firmly to the message that gives life.

PHILIPPIANS 2:15–16 CEV

Believe in the Lord Jesus, and you will be saved—
you and your household.

ACTS 16:31 NIV

[Jesus said,] "You are light for the world. A city cannot be
hidden when it is located on a hill. No one lights a lamp
and puts it under a basket. Instead, everyone who lights
a lamp puts it on a lamp stand. Then its light shines on
everyone in the house. In the same way let your light shine
in front of people. Then they will see the good that you do
and praise your Father in heaven."

MATTHEW 5:14–16 GWT

[Jesus said,] "Plead with the Lord of the harvest to send
out more laborers to help you."

LUKE 10:2 TLB

He wants not only us but everyone saved . . .
to know the truth.

1 TIMOTHY 2:4 MSG

*Pray for your family, walk in love toward them, witness to
them, then leave the rest to God.*

185

THE GREAT THEOLOGIAN and philosopher Thomas Aquinas knew much about education—and even more about motivation. He once said that when you want to convert a person to your view, you should go over to where he is standing, take him by the hand, and guide him to where you are. You shouldn't stand across the room and shout at him. Nor should you threaten him or order him to come over to where you are. Instead, you must start where he is and work from that position, because that's the only way to get people to budge.

Do you have loved ones or family members whom you long to see accept the Good News of Jesus? It is impossible to experience the love, forgiveness, and grace of God without wanting others to know it too. But many times, in our enthusiasm to share our faith with those who are closest to us, we can end up doing more harm than good. Thomas Aquinas's advice still holds true today: A gentle guide is frequently better than a harsh confrontation when you want to convey God's love.

If your greatest prayer is that those whom you love the most would come to know Jesus, rest assured that God hears that prayer. That's His greatest desire, as well. (See 2 Peter 3:9 NKJV.)

Don't give up on your loved ones. Continue to be a

good witness of His love, patience, and understanding. You never know what words or actions God can use to touch their hearts, so be sure to make the most of every opportunity God gives you to be a shining light in their lives.

How is your life a witness of God's love to those around you?

Selfishness

Father in Heaven,

I like to think of myself as a generous person, but the truth is, I am selfish in many ways. Thankfully You are a forgiving God, and I ask You to cleanse me and help me to become more like You.

When I begin to put myself before others or hold on to something instead of being generous, point it out to me so I can change. You gave Your very best, and I want to do the same. Help me to be sensitive to the needs around me so I can be a blessing.

In His name,
Amen.

Do not be selfish or greedy toward your poor brother. But give freely to him. Freely lend him whatever he needs.

DEUTERONOMY 15:7–8 ICB

Don't act out of selfish ambition or be conceited. Instead, humbly think of others as being better than yourselves. Don't be concerned only about your own interests, but also be concerned about the interests of others.

PHILIPPIANS 2:3–4 GWT

Let everyone see that you are unselfish and considerate in all you do. Remember that the Lord is coming soon.

PHILIPPIANS 4:5 TLB

Give to them freely and unselfishly, and the LORD will bless you in everything you do.

DEUTERONOMY 15:10 GNT

Generous gets it all in the end; Stingy is cut off at the pass.

PSALM 37:22 MSG

He that lives not somewhat to others, liveth little to himself.

MICHEL DE MONTAIGNE

HAROLD LUCCOCK, A PASTOR and theologian, once told about a young man who lived and worked in a pretty tough environment. He tried to hold on to his faith, even when people were cruel to him. He was not always appreciated for his religious views, and people often made fun of him. They were always challenging him and his commitment.

One day a particularly abusive person shouted at him, "You fool! Can't you see that if there were a God who cared a penny for the likes of you, He would tell someone to come along and give you what you need—decent food, a bed of your own, at least a chance to make good?"

The young man calmly replied to the man's insult: "I reckon God does tell someone. But someone always forgets."

It's human nature to overlook the needs of others and focus on our own. Someone once summed up this tendency to selfishness this way: "Edith lived in a little world bounded on the north, south, east, and west by Edith."

In contrast to this self-focus, God calls us to die to ourselves and focus our lives on blessing others. Jesus said: "If anyone desires to be My disciple, let him deny himself [disregard, lose sight of, and forget himself and his own interests] and take up his cross and follow Me" (Matthew 16:24 AMP). But in exchange for our giving up our lives for

Him and for others, we receive the blessings of peace, love, and joy in the process. That is definitely a fair trade!

Whom can you bless today?

_____

_____

_____

_____

_____

_____

_____

_____

_____

_____

_____

_____

_____

_____

_____

_____

_____

_____

_____

Sharing My Faith

Heavenly Father,

For many reasons, sharing my faith is often difficult for me, yet I want others to know how good You are. After all, You are the most precious part of my life!

Prepare the hearts of those to whom You want me to witness; then provide opportunities for the subject to be discussed. Embolden me to open my mouth; then fill it with anointed words that will touch the heart. I pray that every seed I sow will bring forth a harvest of souls. With Your help, I can be an effective witness.

In Jesus' name,
Amen.

[Jesus said,] "Do not be worried about how you will defend yourself or what you will say. For the Holy Spirit will teach you at that time what you should say."

Luke 12:11–12 gnt

[Jesus said,] "When the Holy Spirit has come upon you, you will receive power to testify about me with great effect."

Acts 1:8 tlb

We are your servants.
So make us brave enough to speak your message.

Acts 4:29 cev

We have seen and testify to the fact that the Father sent his Son as the Savior of the world. God lives in those who declare that Jesus is the Son of God, and they live in God.

1 John 4:14–15 gwt

We are Christ's ambassadors. God is using us to speak to you: we beg you, as though Christ himself were here pleading with you, receive the love he offers you— be reconciled to God.

2 Corinthians 5:20 tlb

Christians shouldn't be "secret agents."

DO THE PEOPLE AT YOUR JOB know that you're a Christian? How about the people you volunteer with or scrapbook with? Sometimes sharing our faith can be intimidating. We often remain silent for fear of losing the relationship.

But there comes a time when we must be honest about who we are. If we name the name of Christ, we belong to Him. This world is not our home. And we will be held accountable to Him for how we related to others. So how do we begin?

One of the best ways is to pray for the person you'd like to share with. Pray that God will give you a plan of action to reach that person. Also pray for opportunities to share and for courage to take advantage of those opportunities.

Another tactic is to share with people as if they are Christians. A lot of times, we alter our vocabulary when we are with nonbelievers. Don't. If you normally use the phrase "praise the Lord," don't be afraid to say it in front of your friends. If your friends have problems, tell them you'll say a prayer for them. Your vocabulary reveals to them that you are a believer in a nonthreatening way. And they may become curious and ask you questions.

Give them books that appeal to them that also have a Christian message. There are a huge assortment of novels and devotionals to choose from at your local Christian bookstore.

These simple steps help you strengthen your friendship with them, and there's no better way to win them. As you gain their respect as a friend, they will want to hear what you have to say. Why not start today?

What friend would you like to see come to Christ? What are some things you can do to reach her?

_____

_____

_____

_____

_____

_____

_____

_____

_____

_____

_____

Thankfulness

Father in Heaven,

Forgive me for those times when I have been less than thankful and have taken Your blessings for granted. You have been so good to me! Sometimes I get caught up in the busyness of life and forget about Your blessings, or I focus on what I don't have rather than being thankful for what I do have.

I want You to know that I really do appreciate all You have done for me, and I thank You with my whole heart. There is truly no God like You, and I am eternally grateful.

In Jesus' name,
Amen.

God, I will thank you forever for what you have done.
With those who worship you, I will trust you because you
are good.

PSALM 52:9 ICB

I will give thanks to you
because I have been so amazingly and miraculously made.

PSALM 139:14 GWT

Give thanks to the LORD, call on his name;
make known among the nations what he has done.

PSALM 105:1 NIV

Do you see what we've got? An unshakable kingdom! And
do you see how thankful we must be? Not only thankful,
but brimming with worship, deeply reverent before God.

HEBREWS 12:28 MSG

Sing to God with thanksgiving in your hearts. Everything
you do or say, then, should be done in the name of the
Lord Jesus, as you give thanks through him to God the
Father.

COLOSSIANS 3:16–17 GNT

A thankful heart is a happy heart.

✳

ARE YOU THANKFUL? You may be going through some really hard things right now in your life and feel that there is very little to be thankful for. Or your situation may be just the opposite—everything may be going great in your world. Either way, you can still find reasons to be grateful.

Take a few minutes right now and think about all of them. Did you wake up this morning with a roof over your head? Did you have breakfast? Do you have friends and family who love you? Most people have these things so we sometimes take them for granted. But if you answered yes to these questions, you do have a reason to be thankful. Sometimes we are so busy thinking about what we don't have, that we forget to be excited about what we do have.

In the above paragraph, we mentioned the basics, but what about other blessings? What about those cute shoes you found on sale? What about the parking space that was right in front of the store on the day you were so rushed? The Bible says that all good things come from God. (See Matthew 7:11.) God loves us and showers us with blessings each day. Sometimes, we get so focused on our troubles that we fail to see and appreciate all He has done for us.

Why not say thank you to Him right now? Begin to

see your world through the eyes of gratitude. When you begin to count your blessings, they really do multiply!

Make a list of some of your blessings using the letters below.

T _____

_____

H _____

_____

A _____

_____

N _____

_____

K _____

_____

F _____

_____

U _____

_____

L _____

_____

Work

Heavenly Father,

Thank You for my job. Even though I don't always enjoy it, I am grateful to be employed. Help me to approach each day as an opportunity to grow and develop into the person You want me to be. Teach me how to walk in peace and to keep stress at bay.

Open my eyes to creative ideas and solutions, and show me how to accomplish my responsibilities efficiently and with excellence. Finally, I ask You to give me favor with the people I encounter on my job as I do my work unto You.

In Jesus' name,
Amen.

Be ye strong . . . and let not your hands be weak:
for your work shall be rewarded.

2 Chronicles 15:7 KJV

Enjoy the work you do here on earth.
Whatever work you do, do your best.

Ecclesiastes 9:9–10 NCV

A lazy person will end up poor,
but a hard worker will become rich.

Proverbs 10:4 NCV

From the fruit of his lips a man is filled with good things
as surely as the work of his hands rewards him.

Proverbs 12:14 NIV

I think we should enjoy eating, drinking,
and working hard. This is what God intends for us to do.
Suppose you are very rich and able to enjoy everything you
own. Then go ahead and enjoy working hard—
this is God's gift to you.

Ecclesiastes 5:18–19 CEV

*Approaching every day on the job as an opportunity to grow
causes even the most mundane tasks to become stepping-stones
toward fulfilling your destiny.*

SALLY RUSHED TO THE elevator just in time to see the door closing. What a morning! She overslept. She dropped the kids off late for school, and then she spilled coffee on her skirt. And things were about to get worse!

She had no sooner sat down at her desk until she was being called into the boss's office. He informed her that he had hired someone else for the position of office manager, which she had applied for. She was shocked and disappointed. She had been there three years and worked harder than anyone else she knew. Everyone expected her to get the job—this just wasn't fair! She mumbled something and went back to her desk choking back tears.

Later that evening she lay in bed staring at the ceiling. *It just isn't fair,* she kept thinking. Finally, she began to pray and ask the Lord to show her His perspective. He began to calm her heart and gave her an assurance that He would work things out.

Weeks later, Sally met an old friend for lunch. In passing, this friend mentioned a position that was open at her workplace. It just happened to be for an office manager. Sally quickly applied and got the job. Not only was there a slight pay increase, but it was closer to home. How she rejoiced as she looked back to the night that God had spoken peace to her heart.

God can use everyday situations like our jobs to reveal His care and provision. If things aren't going the way you'd like at work, ask God for His wisdom. His plans and His timing are perfect.

What is your biggest complaint about your job? Ask God for a plan of action, and then follow it.

_____

_____

_____

_____

_____

_____

_____

_____

_____

_____

_____

_____

_____

_____

Read through the Bible in a Year Plan

January

1 Genesis 1:1–2:25; Matthew 1:1–2:12; Psalm 1:1–6; Proverbs 1:1–6

2 Genesis 3:1–4:26; Matthew 2:13–3:6; Psalm 2:1–12; Proverbs 1:7–9

3 Genesis 5:1–7:24; Matthew 3:7–4:11; Psalm 3:1–8; Proverbs 1:10–19

4 Genesis 8:1–10:32; Matthew 4:12–25; Psalm 4:1–8; Proverbs 1:20–23

5 Genesis 11:1–13:4; Matthew 5:1–26; Psalm 5:1–12; Proverbs 1:24–28

6 Genesis 13:5–15:21; Matthew 5:27–48; Psalm 6:1–10; Proverbs 1:29–33

7 Genesis 16:1–18:15; Matthew 6:1–24; Psalm 7:1–17; Proverbs 2:1–5

8 Genesis 18:16–19:38; Matthew 6:25–7:14; Psalm 8:1–9; Proverbs 2:6–15

9 Genesis 20:1–22:24; Matthew 7:15–29; Psalm 9:1–12; Proverbs 2:16–22

10 Genesis 23:1–24:51; Matthew 8:1–17; Psalm 9:13–20; Proverbs 3:1–6

11 Genesis 24:52–26:16; Matthew 8:18–34; Psalm 10:1–15; Proverbs 3:7–8

12 Genesis 26:17–27:46; Matthew 9:1–17; Psalm 10:16–18; Proverbs 3:9–10

13 Genesis 28:1–29:35; Matthew 9:18–38; Psalm 11:1–7; Proverbs 3:11–12

14 Genesis 30:1–31:16; Matthew 10:1–23; Psalm 12:1–8; Proverbs 3:13–15

15 Genesis 31:17–32:12; Matthew 10:24–11:6; Psalm 13:1–6; Proverbs 3:16–18

16 Genesis 32:13–34:31; Matthew 11:7–30; Psalm 14:1–7; Proverbs 3:19–20

17 Genesis 35:1–36:43; Matthew 12:1–21; Psalm 15:1–5; Proverbs 3:21–26

18 Genesis 37:1–38:30; Matthew 12:22–45; Psalm 16:1–11; Proverbs 3:27–32

19 Genesis 39:1–41:16; Matthew 12:46–13:23; Psalm 17:1–15; Proverbs 3:33–35

20 Genesis 41:17–42:17; Matthew 13:24–46; Psalm 18:1–15; Proverbs 4:1–6

21 Genesis 42:18–43:34; Matthew 13:47–14:12; Psalm 18:16–36; Proverbs 4:7–10

22 Genesis 44:1–45:28; Matthew 14:13–36; Psalm 18:37–50; Proverbs 4:11–13

23 Genesis 46:1–47:31; Matthew 15:1–28; Psalm 19:1–14; Proverbs 4:14 –19

24 Genesis 48:1–49:33; Matthew 15:29–16:12; Psalm 20:1–9; Proverbs 4:20–27

25 Genesis 50:1–Exodus 2:10; Matthew 16:13–17:9; Psalm 21:1–13; Proverbs 5:1–6

26 Exodus 2:11–3:22; Matthew 17:10–27; Psalm 22:1–18; Proverbs 5:7–14

27 Exodus 4:1–5:21; Matthew 18:1–20; Psalm 22:19–31; Proverbs 5:15–21

28 Exodus 5:22–7:25; Matthew 18:21–19:12; Psalm 23:1–6; Proverbs 5:22–23

29 Exodus 8:1–9:35; Matthew 19:13–30; Psalm 24:1–10; Proverbs 6:1–5

30 Exodus 10:1–12:13; Matthew 20:1–28; Psalm 25:1–15; Proverbs 6:6–11

31 Exodus 12:14–13:16; Matthew 20:29–21:22; Psalm 25:16–22; Proverbs 6:12–15

February

1 Exodus 13:17–15:18; Matthew 21:23–46; Psalm 26:1–12; Proverbs 6:16–19
2 Exodus 15:19–17:7; Matthew 22:1–33; Psalm 27:1–6; Proverbs 6:20–26
3 Exodus 17:8–19:15; Matthew 22:34–23:12; Psalm 27:7–14; Proverbs 6:27–35
4 Exodus 19:16–21:21; Matthew 23:13–39; Psalm 28:1–9; Proverbs 7:1–5
5 Exodus 21:22–23:13; Matthew 24:1–28; Psalm 29:1–11; Proverbs 7:6–23
6 Exodus 23:14–25:40; Matthew 24:29–51; Psalm 30:1–12; Proverbs 7:24–27
7 Exodus 26:1–27:21; Matthew 25:1–30; Psalm 31:1–8; Proverbs 8:1–11
8 Exodus 28:1–43; Matthew 25:31–26:13; Psalm 31:9–18; Proverbs 8:12–13
9 Exodus 29:1–30:10; Matthew 26:14–46; Psalm 31:19–24; Proverbs 8:14–26
10 Exodus 30:11–31:18; Matthew 26:47–68; Psalm 32:1–11; Proverbs 8:27–32
11 Exodus 32:1–33:23; Matthew 26:69–27:14; Psalm 33:1–11; Proverbs 8:33–36
12 Exodus 34:1–35:9; Matthew 27:15–31; Psalm 33:12–22; Proverbs 9:1–6
13 Exodus 35:10–36:38; Matthew 27:32–66; Psalm 34:1–10; Proverbs 9:7–8
14 Exodus 37:1–38:31; Matthew 28:1–20; Psalm 34:11–22; Proverbs 9:9–10
15 Exodus 39:1–40:38; Mark 1:1–28; Psalm 35:1–16; Proverbs 9:11–12
16 Leviticus 1:1–3:17; Mark 1:29–2:12; Psalm 35:17–28; Proverbs 9:13–18
17 Leviticus 4:1–5:19; Mark 2:13–3:6; Psalm 36:1–12; Proverbs 10:1–2
18 Leviticus 6:1–7:27; Mark 3:7–30; Psalm 37:1–11; Proverbs 10:3–4
19 Leviticus 7:28–9:6; Mark 3:31–4:25; Psalm 37:12–29; Proverbs 10:5
20 Leviticus 9:7–10:20; Mark 4:26–5:20; Psalm 37:30–40; Proverbs 10:6–7
21 Leviticus 11:1–12:8; Mark 5:21–43; Psalm 38:1–22; Proverbs 10:8–9
22 Leviticus 13:1–59; Mark 6:1–29; Psalm 39:1–13; Proverbs 10:10
23 Leviticus 14:1–57; Mark 6:30–56; Psalm 40:1–10; Proverbs 10:11–12
24 Leviticus 15:1–16:28; Mark 7:1–23; Psalm 40:11–17; Proverbs 10:13–14
25 Leviticus 16:29–18:30; Mark 7:24–8:10; Psalm 41:1–13; Proverbs 10:15–16
26 Leviticus 19:1–20:21; Mark 8:11–38; Psalm 42:1–11; Proverbs 10:17
27 Leviticus 20:22–22:16; Mark 9:1–29; Psalm 43:1–5; Proverbs 10:18
28 Leviticus 22:17–23:44; Mark 9:30–10:12; Psalm 44:1–8; Proverbs 10:19

March

1 Leviticus 24:1–25:46; Mark 10:13–31; Psalm 44:9–26; Proverbs 10:20–21

2 Leviticus 25:47–27:13; Mark 10:32–52; Psalm 45:1–17; Proverbs 10:22

3 Leviticus 27:14–Numbers 1:54; Mark 11:1–26; Psalm 46:1–11; Proverbs 10:23

4 Numbers 2:1–3:51; Mark 11:27–12:17; Psalm 47:1–9; Proverbs 10:24–25

5 Numbers 4:1–5:31; Mark 12:18–37; Psalm 48:1–14; Proverbs 10:26

6 Numbers 6:1–7:89; Mark 12:38–13:13; Psalm 49:1–20; Proverbs 10:27–28

7 Numbers 8:1–9:23; Mark 13:14–37; Psalm 50:1–23; Proverbs 10:29–30

8 Numbers 10:1–11:23; Mark 14:1–21; Psalm 51:1–19; Proverbs 10:31–32

9 Numbers 11:24–13:33; Mark 14:22–52; Psalm 52:1–9; Proverbs 11:1–3

10 Numbers 14:1–15:16; Mark 14:53–72; Psalm 53:1–6; Proverbs 11:4

11 Numbers 15:17–16:40; Mark 15:1–47; Psalm 54:1–7; Proverbs 11:5–6

12 Numbers 16:41–18:32; Mark 16:1–20; Psalm 55:1–23; Proverbs 11:7

13 Numbers 19:1–20:29; Luke 1:1–25; Psalm 56:1–13; Proverbs 11:8

14 Numbers 21:1–22:20; Luke 1:26–56; Psalm 57:1–11; Proverbs 11:9–11

15 Numbers 22:21–23:30; Luke 1:57–80; Psalm 58:1–11; Proverbs 11:12–13

16 Numbers 24:1–25:18; Luke 2:1–35; Psalm 59:1–17; Proverbs 11:14

17 Numbers 26:1–51; Luke 2:36–52; Psalm 60:1–12; Proverbs 11:15

18 Numbers 26:52–28:15; Luke 3:1–22; Psalm 61:1–8; Proverbs 11:16–17

19 Numbers 28:16–29:40; Luke 3:23–38; Psalm 62:1–12; Proverbs 11:18–19

20 Numbers 30:1–31:54; Luke 4:1–30; Psalm 63:1–11; Proverbs 11:20–21

21 Numbers 32:1–33:39; Luke 4:31–5:11; Psalm 64:1–10; Proverbs 11:22

22 Numbers 33:40–35:34; Luke 5:12–28; Psalm 65:1–13; Proverbs 11:23

23 Numbers 36:1–Deuteronomy 1:46; Luke 5:29–6:11; Psalm 66:1–20; Proverbs 11:24–26

24 Deuteronomy 2:1–3:29; Luke 6:12–38; Psalm 67:1–7; Proverbs 11:27

25 Deuteronomy 4:1–49; Luke 6:39–7:10; Psalm 68:1–18; Proverbs 11:28

26 Deuteronomy 5:1–6:25; Luke 7:11–35; Psalm 68:19–35; Proverbs 11:29–31

27 Deuteronomy 7:1–8:20; Luke 7:36–8:3; Psalm 69:1–18; Proverbs 12:1

28 Deuteronomy 9:1–10:22; Luke 8:4–21; Psalm 69:19–36; Proverbs 12:2–3

29 Deuteronomy 11:1–12:32; Luke 8:22–39; Psalm 70:1–5; Proverbs 12:4

30 Deuteronomy 13:1–15:23; Luke 8:40–9:6; Psalm 71:1–24; Proverbs 12:5–7

31 Deuteronomy 16:1–17:20; Luke 9:7–27; Psalm 72:1–20; Proverbs 12:8–9

April

1 Deuteronomy 18:1–20:20; Luke 9:28–50; Psalm 73:1–28; Proverbs 12:10
2 Deuteronomy 21:1–22:30; Luke 9:51–10:12; Psalm 74:1–23; Proverbs 12:11
3 Deuteronomy 23:1–25:19; Luke 10:13–37; Psalm 75:1–10; Proverbs 12:12–14
4 Deuteronomy 26:1–27:26; Luke 10:38–11:13; Psalm 76:1–12; Proverbs 12:15–17
5 Deuteronomy 28:1–68; Luke 11:14–36; Psalm 77:1–20; Proverbs 12:18
6 Deuteronomy 29:1–30:20; Luke 11:37–12:7; Psalm 78:1–31; Proverbs 12:19–20
7 Deuteronomy 31:1–32:27; Luke 12:8–34; Psalm 78:32–55; Proverbs 12:21–23
8 Deuteronomy 32:28–52; Luke 12:35–59; Psalm 78:56–64; Proverbs 12:24
9 Deuteronomy 33:1–29; Luke 13:1–21; Psalm 78:65–72; Proverbs 12:25
10 Deuteronomy 34:1–Joshua 2:24; Luke 13:22–14:6; Psalm 79:1–13; Proverbs 12:26
11 Joshua 3:1–4:24; Luke 14:7–35; Psalm 80:1–19; Proverbs 12:27–28
12 Joshua 5:1–7:15; Luke 15:1–32; Psalm 81:1–16; Proverbs 13:1
13 Joshua 7:16–9:2; Luke 16:1–18; Psalm 82:1–8; Proverbs 13:2–3
14 Joshua 9:3–10:43; Luke 16:19–17:10; Psalm 83:1–18; Proverbs 13:4
15 Joshua 11:1–12:24; Luke 17:11–37; Psalm 84:1–12; Proverbs 13:5–6
16 Joshua 13:1–14:15; Luke 18:1–17; Psalm 85:1–13; Proverbs 13:7–8
17 Joshua 15:1–63; Luke 18:18–43; Psalm 86:1–17; Proverbs 13:9–10
18 Joshua 16:1–18:28; Luke 19:1–27; Psalm 87:1–7; Proverbs 13:11
19 Joshua 19:1–20:9; Luke 19:28–48; Psalm 88:1–18; Proverbs 13:12–14
20 Joshua 21:1–22:20; Luke 20:1–26; Psalm 89:1–13; Proverbs 13:15–16
21 Joshua 22:21–23:16; Luke 20:27–47; Psalm 89:14–37; Proverbs 13:17–19
22 Joshua 24:1–33; Luke 21:1–28; Psalm 89:38–52; Proverbs 13:20–23
23 Judges 1:1–2:9; Luke 21:29–22:13; Psalm 90:1–91:16; Proverbs 13:24–25
24 Judges 2:10–3:31; Luke 22:14–34; Psalm 92:1–93:5; Proverbs 14:1–2
25 Judges 4:1–5:31; Luke 22:35–53; Psalm 94:1–23; Proverbs 14:3–4
26 Judges 6:1–40; Luke 22:54–23:12; Psalm 95:1–96:13; Proverbs 14:5–6
27 Judges 7:1–8:17; Luke 23:13–43; Psalm 97:1–98:9; Proverbs 14:7–8
28 Judges 8:18–9:21; Luke 23:44–24:12; Psalm 99:1–9; Proverbs 14:9–10
29 Judges 9:22–10:18; Luke 24:13–53; Psalm 100:1–5; Proverbs 14:11–12
30 Judges 11:1–12:15; John 1:1–28; Psalm 101:1–8; Proverbs 14:13–14

May

1 Judges 13:1–14:20; John 1:29–51; Psalm 102:1–28; Proverbs 14:15–16
2 Judges 15:1–16:31; John 2:1–25; Psalm 103:1–22; Proverbs 14:17–19
3 Judges 17:1–18:31; John 3:1–21; Psalm 104:1–23; Proverbs 14:20–21
4 Judges 19:1–20:48; John 3:22–4:3; Psalm 104:24–35; Proverbs 14:22–24
5 Judges 21:1–Ruth 1:22; John 4:4–42; Psalm 105:1–15; Proverbs 14:25
6 Ruth 2:1–4:22; John 4:43–54; Psalm 105:16–36; Proverbs 14:26–27
7 1 Samuel 1:1–2:21; John 5:1–23; Psalm 105:37–45; Proverbs 14:28–29
8 1 Samuel 2:22–4:22; John 5:24–47; Psalm 106:1–12; Proverbs 14:30–31
9 1 Samuel 5:1–7:17; John 6:1–21; Psalm 106:13–31; Proverbs 14:32–33
10 1 Samuel 8:1–9:27; John 6:22–42; Psalm 106:32–48; Proverbs 14:34–35
11 1 Samuel 10:1–11:15; John 6:43–71; Psalm 107:1–43; Proverbs 15:1–3
12 1 Samuel 12:1–13:23; John 7:1–30; Psalm 108:1–13; Proverbs 15:4
13 1 Samuel 14:1–52; John 7:31–53; Psalm 109:1–31; Proverbs 15:5–7
14 1 Samuel 15:1–16:23; John 8:1–20; Psalm 110:1–7; Proverbs 15:8–10
15 1 Samuel 17:1–18:4; John 8:21–30; Psalm 111:1–10; Proverbs 15:11
16 1 Samuel 18:5–19:24; John 8:31–59; Psalm 112:1–10; Proverbs 15:12–14
17 1 Samuel 20:1–21:15; John 9:1–41; Psalm 113:1–114:8; Proverbs 15:15–17
18 1 Samuel 22:1–23:29; John 10:1–21; Psalm 115:1–18; Proverbs 15:18–19
19 1 Samuel 24:1–25:44; John 10:22–42; Psalm 116:1–19; Proverbs 15:20–21
20 1 Samuel 26:1–28:25; John 11:1–54; Psalm 117:1–2; Proverbs 15:22–23
21 1 Samuel 29:1–31:13; John 11: 55–12:19; Psalm 118:1–18; Proverbs 15:24–26
22 2 Samuel 1:1–2:11; John 12:20–50; Psalm 118:19–29: Proverbs 15:27–28
23 2 Samuel 2:12–3:39; John 13:1–30; Psalm 119:1–16; Proverbs 15:29–30
24 2 Samuel 4:1–6:23; John 13:31–14:14; Psalm 119:17–32; Proverbs 15:31–32
25 2 Samuel 7:1–8:18; John 14:15–31; Psalm 119:33–48; Proverbs 15:33
26 2 Samuel 9:1–11:27; John 15:1–27; Psalm 119:49–64; Proverbs 16:1–3
27 2 Samuel 12:1–31; John 16:1–33; Psalm 119:65–80; Proverbs 16:4–5
28 2 Samuel 13:1–39; John 17:1–26; Psalm 119:81–96; Proverbs 16:6–7
29 2 Samuel 14:1–15:22; John 18:1–24; Psalm 119:97–112; Proverbs 16:8–9
30 2 Samuel 15:23–16:23; John 18:25–19:22; Psalm 119:113–128; Proverbs 16:10–11
31 2 Samuel 17:1–29; John 19:23–42; Psalm 119:129–152; Proverbs 16:12–13

June

1 2 Samuel 18:1–19:10; John 20:1–31; Psalm 119:153–176; Proverbs 16:14–15
2 2 Samuel 19:11–20:13; John 21:1–25; Psalm 120:1–7; Proverbs 16:16–17
3 2 Samuel 20:14–21:22; Acts 1:1–26; Psalm 121:1– 8; Proverbs 16:18
4 2 Samuel 22:1–23:2; Acts 2:1–47; Psalm 122:1–9; Proverbs 16:19–20
5 2 Samuel 23:3–24:25; Acts 3:1–26; Psalm 123:1–4; Proverbs 16:21–23
6 1 Kings 1:1–53; Acts 4:1–37; Psalm 124:1–8; Proverbs 16:24
7 1 Kings 2:1–3:2; Acts 5:1–42; Psalm 125:1–5; Proverbs 16:25
8 1 Kings 3:3–4:34; Acts 6:1–15; Psalm 126:1–6; Proverbs 16:26–27
9 1 Kings 5:1–6:38; Acts 7:1–29; Psalm 127:1–5; Proverbs 16:28–30
10 1 Kings 7:1–51; Acts 7:30–50; Psalm 128:1–6; Proverbs 16:31–33
11 1 Kings 8:1–66; Acts 7:51–8:13; Psalm 129:1–8; Proverbs 17:1
12 1 Kings 9:1–10:29; Acts 8:14–40; Psalm 130:1–8; Proverbs 17:2–3
13 1 Kings 11:1–12:19; Acts 9:1–25; Psalm 131:1–3; Proverbs 17:4–5
14 1 Kings 12:20–13:34; Acts 9:26–43; Psalm 132:1–18; Proverbs 17:6
15 1 Kings 14:1–15:24; Acts 10:1:23; Psalm 133:1–3; Proverbs 17:7–8
16 1 Kings 15:25–17:24; Acts 10:24–48; Psalm 134:1–3; Proverbs 17:9–11
17 1 Kings 18:1–46; Acts 11:1–30; Psalm 135:1–21; Proverbs 17:12–13
18 1 Kings 19:1–21; Acts 12:1–23; Psalm 136:1–26; Proverbs 17:14–15
19 1 Kings 20:1–21:29; Acts 12:24–13:15; Psalm 137:1–9; Proverbs 17:16
20 1 Kings 22:1–53; Acts 13:16–41; Psalm 138:1–8; Proverbs 17:17–18
21 2 Kings 1:1–2:25; Acts 13:42–14:7; Psalm 139:1–24; Proverbs 17:19–21
22 2 Kings 3:1–4:17; Acts 14:8–28; Psalm 140:1–13; Proverbs 17:22
23 2 Kings 4:18–5:27; Acts 15:1–35; Psalm 141:1–10; Proverbs 17:23
24 2 Kings 6:1–7:20; Acts 15:36–16:15; Psalm 142:1–7; Proverbs 17:24–25
25 2 Kings 8:1–9:13; Acts 16:16–40; Psalm 143:1–12; Proverbs 17:26
26 2 Kings 9:14–10:31; Acts 17:1–34; Psalm 144:1–15; Proverbs 17:27–28
27 2 Kings 10:32–12:21; Acts 18:1–22; Psalm 145:1–21; Proverbs 18:1
28 2 Kings 13:1–14:29; Acts 18:23–19:12; Psalm 146:1–10; Proverbs 18:2–3
29 2 Kings 15:1–16:20; Acts 19:13–41; Psalm 147:1–20; Proverbs 18:4–5
30 2 Kings 17:1–18:12; Acts 20:1–38; Psalm 148:1–14; Proverbs 18:6–7

July

1 2 Kings 18:13–19:37; Acts 21:1–17; Psalm 149:1–9; Proverbs 18:8
2 2 Kings 20:1–22:2; Acts 21:18–36; Psalm 150:1–6; Proverbs 18:9–10
3 2 Kings 22:3–23:30; Acts 21:37–22:16; Psalm 1:1–6; Proverbs 18:11–12
4 2 Kings 23:31–25:30; Acts 22:17–23:10; Psalm 2:1–12; Proverbs 18:13
5 1 Chronicles 1:1–2:17; Acts 23:11–35; Psalm 3:1–8; Proverbs 18:14–15
6 1 Chronicles 2:18–4:4; Acts 24:1–27; Psalm 4:1–8; Proverbs 18:16–18
7 1 Chronicles 4:5–5:17; Acts 25:1–27; Psalm 5:1–12; Proverbs 18:19
8 1 Chronicles 5:18–6:81; Acts 26:1–32; Psalm 6:1–10; Proverbs 18:20–21
9 1 Chronicles 7:1–8:40; Acts 27:1–20; Psalm 7:1–17; Proverbs 18:22
10 1 Chronicles 9:1–10:14; Acts 27:21–44; Psalm 8:1–9; Proverbs 18:23–24
11 1 Chronicles 11:1–12:18; Acts 28:1–31; Psalm 9:1–12; Proverbs 19:1–3
12 1 Chronicles 12:19–14:17; Romans 1:1–17; Psalm 9:13–20; Proverbs 19:4–5
13 1 Chronicles 15:1–16:36; Romans 1:18–32; Psalm 10:1–15; Proverbs 19:6–7
14 1 Chronicles 16:37–18:17; Romans 2:1–24; Psalm 10:16–18; Proverbs 19:8–9
15 1 Chronicles 19:1–21:30; Romans 2:25–3:8; Psalm 11:1–7; Proverbs 19:10–12
16 1 Chronicles 22:1–23:32; Romans 3:9–31; Psalm 12:1–8; Proverbs 19:13–14
17 1 Chronicles 24:1–26:11; Romans 4:1–12; Psalm 13:1–6; Proverbs 19:15–16
18 1 Chronicles 26:12–27:34; Romans 4:13–5:5; Psalm 14:1–7; Proverbs 19:17
19 1 Chronicles 28:1–29:30; Romans 5:6–21; Psalm 15:1–5; Proverbs 19:18–19
20 2 Chronicles 1:1–3:17; Romans 6:1–23; Psalm 16:1–11; Proverbs 19:20–21
21 2 Chronicles 4:1–6:11; Romans 7:1–13; Psalm 17:1–15; Proverbs 19:22–23
22 2 Chronicles 6:12–8:10; Romans 7:14–8:8; Psalm 18:1–15; Proverbs 19:24–25
23 2 Chronicles 8:11–10:19; Romans 8:9–25; Psalm 18:16–36; Proverbs 19:26
24 2 Chronicles 11:1–13:22; Romans 8:26–39; Psalm 18:37–50; Proverbs 19:27–29
25 2 Chronicles 14:1–16:14; Romans 9:1–24; Psalm 19:1–14; Proverbs 20:1
26 2 Chronicles 17:1–18:34; Romans 9:25–10:13; Psalm 20:1–9; Proverbs 20:2–3
27 2 Chronicles 19:1–20:37; Romans 10:14–11:12; Psalm 21:1–13; Proverbs 20:4–6
28 2 Chronicles 21:1–23:21; Romans 11:13–36; Psalm 22:1–18; Proverbs 20:7
29 2 Chronicles 24:1–25:28; Romans 12:1–21; Psalm 22:19–31; Proverbs 20:8–10
30 2 Chronicles 26:1–28:27; Romans 13:1–14; Psalm 23:1–6; Proverbs 20:11
31 2 Chronicles 29:1–36; Romans 14:1–23; Psalm 24:1–10; Proverbs 20:12

August

1 2 Chronicles 30:1–31:21; Romans 15:1–22; Psalm 25:1–15; Proverbs 20:13–15
2 2 Chronicles 32:1–33:13; Romans 15:23–16:9; Psalm 25:16–22; Proverbs 20:16–18
3 2 Chronicles 33:14–34:33; Romans 16:10–27; Psalm 26:1–12; Proverbs 20:19
4 2 Chronicles 35:1–36:23; 1 Corinthians 1:1–17; Psalm 27:1–6; Proverbs 20:20–21
5 Ezra 1:1–2:70; 1 Corinthians 1:18–2:5; Psalm 27:7–14; Proverbs 20:22–23
6 Ezra 3:1–4:23; 1 Corinthians 2:6–3:4; Psalm 28:1–9; Proverbs 20:24–25
7 Ezra 4:24–6:22; 1 Corinthians 3:5–23; Psalm 29:1–11; Proverbs 20:26–27
8 Ezra 7:1–8:20; 1 Corinthians 4:1–21; Psalm 30:1–12; Proverbs 20:28–30
9 Ezra 8:21–9:15; 1 Corinthians 5:1–13; Psalm 31:1–8; Proverbs 21:1–2
10 Ezra 10:1–44; 1 Corinthians 6:1–20; Psalm 31:9–18; Proverbs 21:3
11 Nehemiah 1:1–3:14; 1 Corinthians 7:1–24; Psalm 31:19–24; Proverbs 21:4
12 Nehemiah 3:15–5:13; 1 Corinthians 7:25–40; Psalm 32:1–11; Proverbs 21:5–7
13 Nehemiah 5:14–7:73; 1 Corinthians 8:1–13; Psalm 33:1–11; Proverbs 21:8–10
14 Nehemiah 8:1–9:21; 1 Corinthians 9:1–18; Psalm 33:12–22; Proverbs 21:11–12
15 Nehemiah 9:22–10:39; 1 Corinthians 9:19–10:13; Psalm 34:1–10; Proverbs 21:13
16 Nehemiah 11:1–12:26; 1 Corinthians 10:14–33; Psalm 34:11–22; Proverbs 21:14–16
17 Nehemiah 12:27–13:31; 1 Corinthians 11:1–16; Psalm 35:1–16; Proverbs 21:17–18
18 Esther 1:1–3:15; 1 Corinthians 11:17–34; Psalm 35:17–28; Proverbs 21:19–20
19 Esther 4:1–7:10; 1 Corinthians 12:1–26; Psalm 36:1–12; Proverbs 21:21–22
20 Esther 8:1–10:3; 1 Corinthians 12:27–13:13; Psalm 37:1–11; Proverbs 21:23–24
21 Job 1:1–3:26; 1 Corinthians 14:1–17; Psalm 37:12–29; Proverbs 21:25–26
22 Job 4:1–7:21; 1 Corinthians 14:18–40; Psalm 37:30–40; Proverbs 21:27
23 Job 8:1–11:20; 1 Corinthians 15:1–28; Psalm 38:1–22; Proverbs 21:28–29
24 Job 12:1–15:35; 1 Corinthians 15:29–58; Psalm 39:1–13; Proverbs 21:30–31
25 Job 16:1–19:29; 1 Corinthians 16:1–24; Psalm 40:1–10; Proverbs 22:1
26 Job 20:1–22:30; 2 Corinthians 1:1–11; Psalm 40:11–17; Proverbs 22:2–4
27 Job 23:1–27:23; 2 Corinthians 1:12–2:11; Psalm 41:1–13; Proverbs 22:5–6
28 Job 28:1–30:31; 2 Corinthians 2:12–17; Psalm 42:1–11; Proverbs 22:7
29 Job 31:1–33:33; 2 Corinthians 3:1–18; Psalm 43:1–5; Proverbs 22:8–9
30 Job 34:1–36:33; 2 Corinthians 4:1–12; Psalm 44:1–8; Proverbs 22:10–12
31 Job 37:1–39:30; 2 Corinthians 4:13–5:10; Psalm 44:9–26; Proverbs 22:13

September

1 Job 40:1–42:17; 2 Corinthians 5:11–21; Psalm 45:1–17; Proverbs 22:14

2 Ecclesiastes 1:1–3:22; 2 Corinthians 6:1–13; Psalm 46:1–11; Proverbs 22:15

3 Ecclesiastes 4:1–6:12; 2 Corinthians 6:14–7:7; Psalm 47:1–9; Proverbs 22:16

4 Ecclesiastes 7:1–9:18; 2 Corinthians 7:8–16; Psalm 48:1–14; Proverbs 22:17–19

5 Ecclesiastes 10:1–12:14; 2 Corinthians 8:1–15; Psalm 49:1–20; Proverbs 22:20–21

6 Song of Solomon 1:1–4:16; 2 Corinthians 8:16–24; Psalm 50:1–23; Proverbs 22:22–23

7 Song of Solomon 5:1–8:14; 2 Corinthians 9:1–15; Psalm 51:1–19; Proverbs 22:24–25

8 Isaiah 1:1–2:22; 2 Corinthians 10:1–18; Psalm 52:1–9; Proverbs 22:26–27

9 Isaiah 3:1–5:30; 2 Corinthians 11:1–15; Psalm 53:1–6; Proverbs 22:28–29

10 Isaiah 6:1–7:25: 2 Corinthians 11:16–33; Psalm 54:1–7; Proverbs 23:1–3

11 Isaiah 8:1–9:21; 2 Corinthians 12:1–10; Psalm 55:1–23; Proverbs 23:4–5

12 Isaiah 10:1–11:16; 2 Corinthians 12:11–21; Psalm 56:1–13; Proverbs 23:6–8

13 Isaiah 12:1–14:32; 2 Corinthians 13:1–14; Psalm 57:1–11; Proverbs 23:9–11

14 Isaiah 15:1–18:7; Galatians 1:1–24; Psalm 58:1–11; Proverbs 23:12

15 Isaiah 19:1–21:17; Galatians 2:1–16; Psalm 59:1–17; Proverbs 23:13–14

16 Isaiah 22:1–24:23; Galatians 2:17–3:9; Psalm 60:1–12; Proverbs 23:15–16

17 Isaiah 25:1–28:13; Galatians 3:10–22; Psalm 61:1–8; Proverbs 23:17–18

18 Isaiah 28:14–30:11; Galatians 3:23–4:31; Psalm 62:1–12; Proverbs 23:19–21

19 Isaiah 30:12–33:9; Galatians 5:1–12; Psalm 63:1–11; Proverbs 23:22

20 Isaiah 33:10–36:22; Galatians 5:13–26; Psalm 64:1–10; Proverbs 23:23

21 Isaiah 37:1–38:22; Galatians 6:1–18; Psalm 65:1–13; Proverbs 23:24

22 Isaiah 39:1–41:16; Ephesians 1:1–23; Psalm 66:1–20; Proverbs 23:25–28

23 Isaiah 41:17–43:13; Ephesians 2:1–22; Psalm 67:1–7; Proverbs 23:29–35

24 Isaiah 43:14–45:10; Ephesians 3:1–21; Psalm 68:1–18; Proverbs 24:1–2

25 Isaiah 45:11–48:11; Ephesians 4:1–16; Psalm 68:19–35; Proverbs 24:3–4

26 Isaiah 48:12–50:11; Ephesians 4:17–32; Psalm 69:1–18; Proverbs 24:5–6

27 Isaiah 51:1–53:12; Ephesians 5:1–33; Psalm 69:19–36; Proverbs 24:7

28 Isaiah 54:1–57:14; Ephesians 6:1–24; Psalm 70:1–5; Proverbs 24:8

29 Isaiah 57:15–59:21; Philippians 1:1–26; Psalm 71:1–24; Proverbs 24:9–10

30 Isaiah 60:1–62:5; Philippians 1:27–2:18; Psalm 72:1–20; Proverbs 24:11–12

October

1 Isaiah 62:6–65:25; Philippians 2:19–3:3; Psalm 73:1–28; Proverbs 24:13–14
2 Isaiah 66:1–24; Philippians 3:4–21; Psalm 74:1–23; Proverbs 24:15–16
3 Jeremiah 1:1–2:30; Philippians 4:1–23; Psalm 75:1–10; Proverbs 24:17–20
4 Jeremiah 2:31–4:18; Colossians 1:1–17; Psalm 76:1–12; Proverbs 24:21–22
5 Jeremiah 4:19–6:15; Colossians 1:18–2:7; Psalm 77:1–20; Proverbs 24:23–25
6 Jeremiah 6:16–8:7; Colossians 2:8–23; Psalm 78:1–31; Proverbs 24:26
7 Jeremiah 8:8–9:26; Colossians 3:1–17; Psalm 78:32–55; Proverbs 24:27
8 Jeremiah 10:1–11:23; Colossians 3:18–4:18; Psalm 78:56–72; Proverbs 24:28–29
9 Jeremiah 12:1–14:10; 1 Thessalonians 1:1–2:8; Psalm 79:1–13; Proverbs 24:30–34
10 Jeremiah 14:11–16:15; 1 Thessalonians 2:9–3:13; Psalm 80:1–19; Proverbs 25:1–5
11 Jeremiah 16:16–18:23; 1 Thessalonians 4:1–5:3; Psalm 81:1–16; Proverbs 25:6–8
12 Jeremiah 19:1–21:14; 1 Thessalonians 5:4–28; Psalm 82:1–8; Proverbs 25:9–10
13 Jeremiah 22:1–23:20; 2 Thessalonians 1:1–12; Psalm 83:1–18; Proverbs 25:11–14
14 Jeremiah 23:21–25:38; 2 Thessalonians 2:1–17; Psalm 84:1–12; Proverbs 25:15
15 Jeremiah 26:1–27:22; 2 Thessalonians 3:1–18; Psalm 85:1–13; Proverbs 25:16
16 Jeremiah 28:1–29:32; 1 Timothy 1:1–20; Psalm 86:1–17; Proverbs 25:17
17 Jeremiah 30:1–31:26; 1 Timothy 2:1–15; Psalm 87:1–7; Proverbs 25:18–19
18 Jeremiah 31:27–32:44; 1 Timothy 3:1–16; Psalm 88:1–18; Proverbs 25:20–22
19 Jeremiah 33:1–34:22; 1 Timothy 4:1–16; Psalm 89:1–13; Proverbs 25:23–24
20 Jeremiah 35:1–36:32; 1 Timothy 5:1–25; Psalm 89:14–37; Proverbs 25:25–27
21 Jeremiah 37:1–38:28; 1 Timothy 6:1–21; Psalm 89:38–52; Proverbs 25:28
22 Jeremiah 39:1–41:18; 2 Timothy 1:1–18; Psalm 90:1–91:16; Proverbs 26:1–2
23 Jeremiah 42:1–44:23; 2 Timothy 2:1–21; Psalm 92:1–93:5; Proverbs 26:3–5
24 Jeremiah 44:24–47:7; 2 Timothy 2:22–3:17; Psalm 94:1–23; Proverbs 26:6–8
25 Jeremiah 48:1–49:22; 2 Timothy 4:1–22; Psalm 95:1–96:13; Proverbs 26:9–12
26 Jeremiah 49:23–50:46; Titus 1:1–16; Psalm 97:1–98:9; Proverbs 26:13–16
27 Jeremiah 51:1–53; Titus 2:1–15; Psalm 99:1–9; Proverbs 26:17
28 Jeremiah 51:54–52:34; Titus 3:1–15; Psalm 100:1–5; Proverbs 26:18–19
29 Lamentations 1:1–2:22; Philemon 1:1–25; Psalm 101:1–8; Proverbs 26:20
30 Lamentations 3:1–66; Hebrews 1:1–14; Psalm 102:1–28; Proverbs 26:21–22
31 Lamentations 4:1–5:22; Hebrews 2:1–18; Psalm 103:1–22; Proverbs 26:23

November

1 Ezekiel 1:1–3:15; Hebrews 3:1–19; Psalm 104:1–23; Proverbs 26:24–26
2 Ezekiel 3:16–6:14; Hebrews 4:1–16; Psalm 104:24–35; Proverbs 26:27
3 Ezekiel 7:1–9:11; Hebrews 5:1–14; Psalm 105:1–15; Proverbs 26:28
4 Ezekiel 10:1–11:25; Hebrews 6:1–20; Psalm 105:16–36; Proverbs 27:1–2
5 Ezekiel 12:1–14:11; Hebrews 7:1–17; Psalm 105:37–45; Proverbs 27:3
6 Ezekiel 14:12–16:41; Hebrews 7:18–28; Psalm 106:1–12; Proverbs 27:4–6
7 Ezekiel 16:42–17:24; Hebrews 8:1–13; Psalm 106:13–31; Proverbs 27:7–9
8 Ezekiel 18:1–19:14; Hebrews 9:1–10; Psalm 106:32–48; Proverbs 27:10
9 Ezekiel 20:1–49; Hebrews 9:11–28; Psalm 107:1–43; Proverbs 27:11
10 Ezekiel 21:1–22:31; Hebrews 10:1–17; Psalm 108:1–13; Proverbs 27:12
11 Ezekiel 23:1–49; Hebrews 10:18–39; Psalm 109:1–31; Proverbs 27:13
12 Ezekiel 24:1–26:21; Hebrews 11:1–16; Psalm 110:1–7; Proverbs 27:14
13 Ezekiel 27:1–28:26; Hebrews 11:17–31; Psalm 111:1–10; Proverbs 27:15–16
14 Ezekiel 29:1–30:26; Hebrews 11:32–12:13; Psalm 112:1–10; Proverbs 27:17
15 Ezekiel 31:1–32:32; Hebrews 12:14–29; Psalm 113:1–114:8; Proverbs 27:18–20
16 Ezekiel 33:1–34:31; Hebrews 13:1–25; Psalm 115:1–18; Proverbs 27:21–22
17 Ezekiel 35:1–36:38; James 1:1–18; Psalm 116:1–19; Proverbs 27:23–27
18 Ezekiel 37:1–38:23; James 1:19–2:17; Psalm 117:1–2; Proverbs 28:1
19 Ezekiel 39:1–40:27; James 2:18–3:18; Psalm 118:1–18; Proverbs 28:2
20 Ezekiel 40:28–41:26; James 4:1–17; Psalm 118:19–29; Proverbs 28:3–5
21 Ezekiel 42:1–43:27; James 5:1–20; Psalm 119:1–16; Proverbs 28:6–7
22 Ezekiel 44:1–45:12; 1 Peter 1:1–12; Psalm 119:17–32; Proverbs 28:8–10
23 Ezekiel 45:13–46:24; 1 Peter 1:13–2:10; Psalm 119:33–48; Proverbs 28:11
24 Ezekiel 47:1–48:35; 1 Peter 2:11–3:7; Psalm 119:49–64; Proverbs 28:12–13
25 Daniel 1:1–2:23; 1 Peter 3:8–4:6; Psalm 119:65–80; Proverbs 28:14
26 Daniel 2:24–3:30; 1 Peter 4:7–5:14; Psalm 119:81–96; Proverbs 28:15–16
27 Daniel 4:1–37; 2 Peter 1:1–21; Psalm 119:97–112; Proverbs 28:17–18
28 Daniel 5:1–31; 2 Peter 2:1–22; Psalm 119:113–128; Proverbs 28:19–20
29 Daniel 6:1–28; 2 Peter 3:1–18; Psalm 119:129–152; Proverbs 28:21–22
30 Daniel 7:1–28; 1 John 1:1–10; Psalm 119:153–176; Proverbs 28:23–24

December

1 Daniel 8:1–27; 1 John 2:1–17; Psalm 120:1–7; Proverbs 28:25–26

2 Daniel 9:1–11:1; 1 John 2:18–3:6; Psalm 121:1–8; Proverbs 28:27–28

3 Daniel 11:2–35; 1 John 3:7–24; Psalm 122:1–9; Proverbs 29:1

4 Daniel 11:36–12:13; 1 John 4:1–21; Psalm 123:1–4; Proverbs 29:2–4

5 Hosea 1:1–3:5; 1 John 5:1–21; Psalm 124:1–8; Proverbs 29:5–8

6 Hosea 4:1–5:15; 2 John 1:1–13; Psalm 125:1–5; Proverbs 29:9–11

7 Hosea 6:1–9:17; 3 John 1:1–15; Psalm 126:1–6; Proverbs 29:12–14

8 Hosea 10:1–14:9; Jude 1:1–25; Psalm 127:1–5; Proverbs 29:15–17

9 Joel 1:1–3:21; Revelation 1:1–20; Psalm 128:1–6; Proverbs 29:18

10 Amos 1:1–3:15; Revelation 2:1–17; Psalm 129:1–8; Proverbs 29:19–20

11 Amos 4:1–6:14; Revelation 2:18–3:6; Psalm 130:1–8; Proverbs 29:21–22

12 Amos 7:1–9:15; Revelation 3:7–22; Psalm 131:1–3; Proverbs 29:23

13 Obadiah 1:1–21; Revelation 4:1–11; Psalm 132:1–18; Proverbs 29:24–25

14 Jonah 1:1–4:11; Revelation 5:1–14; Psalm 133:1–3; Proverbs 29:26–27

15 Micah 1:1–4:13; Revelation 6:1–17; Psalm 134:1–3; Proverbs 30:1–4

16 Micah 5:1–7:20; Revelation 7:1–17; Psalm 135:1–21; Proverbs 30:5–6

17 Nahum 1:1–3:19; Revelation 8:1–13; Psalm 136:1–26; Proverbs 30:7–9

18 Habakkuk 1:1–3:19; Revelation 9:1–21; Psalm 137:1–9; Proverbs 30:10

19 Zephaniah 1:1–3:20; Revelation 10:1–11; Psalm 138:1–8; Proverbs 30:11–14

20 Haggai 1:1–2:23; Revelation 11:1–19; Psalm 139:1–24; Proverbs 30:15–16

21 Zechariah 1:1–21; Revelation 12:1–17; Psalm 140:1–13; Proverbs 30:17

22 Zechariah 2:1–3:10; Revelation 13:1–18; Psalm 141:1–10; Proverbs 30:18–20

23 Zechariah 4:1–5:11; Revelation 14:1–20; Psalm 142:1–7; Proverbs 30:21–23

24 Zechariah 6:1–7:14; Revelation 15:1–8; Psalm 143:1–12; Proverbs 30:24–28

25 Zechariah 8:1–23; Revelation 16:1–21; Psalm 144:1–15; Proverbs 30:29–31

26 Zechariah 9:1–17; Revelation 17:1–18; Psalm 145:1–21; Proverbs 30:32

27 Zechariah 10:1–11:17; Revelation 18:1–24; Psalm 146:1–10; Proverbs 30:33

28 Zechariah 12:1–13:9; Revelation 19:1–21; Psalm 147:1–20; Proverbs 31:1–7

29 Zechariah 14:1–21; Revelation 20:1–15; Psalm 148:1–14; Proverbs 31:8–9

30 Malachi 1:1–2:17; Revelation 21:1–27; Psalm 149:1–9; Proverbs 31:10–24

31 Malachi 3:1–4:6; Revelation 22:1–21; Psalm 150:1–6; Proverbs 31:25–31

Also look for *My Pocket Prayer Partner for Moms.*